Religion
AND THE LIFE CYCLE

Religion
AND THE
LIFE CYCLE

ROBERT C. FULLER

FORTRESS PRESS   PHILADELPHIA

Library of Congress Cataloging-in-Publication Data

Fuller, Robert C., 1952–
　Religion and the life cycle.

　Bibliography: p.
　1. Religion.　2. Psychology, Religious.　3. Life cycle, Human.　I. Title.
　BL48.F86 1988　　200'.1'9　　88–45237
　ISBN 0–8006–2306–1

3448C87　Printed in the United States of America　1–2306

To Bryan

CONTENTS

Preface   ix

Introduction   1

1. Religion and Childhood Development   14

2. Belief and Identity Formation   34

3. Values and Midlife Transitions   56

4. Aging, Dying, and Integrity   74

5. Religion and Self-transcendence   96

6. Religion and the Art of Life Cycle Maintenance   116

Epilogue   136

Notes   141

Suggested Reading   149

Index   155

PREFACE

This book is intended to help modern, educated individuals think about the value of religion. Its goal is to contribute to the philosophy of religion, drawing on and in dialogue with psychological perspectives on human fulfillment. The book was written as a kind of sequel to Gordon Allport's classic study of religion entitled *The Individual and His Religion.* Allport's text, now nearly forty years old, introduced a mode of discussing the role of religion in personal life that deserves renewal and further development. It is my hope that this book will engage readers anew in the complex process of assessing the origin and function of religion in human experience.

This book emerged out of a very successful course I have taught to both undergraduate students at Bradley University and graduate students at the University of Chicago. I have intended the book to serve the dual goals of providing peers with a helpful professional reference volume and offering students or lay persons a readable introduction to the psychological study of religion. I wish to make it clear that I take seriously my responsibilities as an author to help introductory-level readers understand the kinds of inquiry that characterize the academic study of religion. Persons experienced in this field will find some sections that are fairly elementary and cover material already well-known in their professional discipline. I only hope that they will appreciate that the textbookish nature of these sections is precisely what will enable them to use the text to introduce colleagues and students to issues raised by this kind of inquiry into religion.

A few caveats: My use of life cycle theories of psychological development is primarily for the purpose of organization and to open up a certain hermeneutical style for assessing the nature and meaning of religion. The text does not intend to engage in critical revision of these theories; nor does it wish slavishly to restrict its discussion of the psychological functions of religion to life cycle themes (particularly in chap. 6). And, finally, there is a certain Western and Christian bias in this book. Given that most of the potential readers of this book will be from Western and Christian backgrounds, this struck the author as both justified and appropriate.

The early work on this manuscript was begun during the final weeks of my fellowship at the Institute for the Advanced Study of Religion at the University of Chicago. I would like to thank the Institute's staff for their hospitality. I would also like to thank Brooks McDaniel, a colleague at nearby Illinois Community College, for reading an early draft of this manuscript and helping me think through the issues that arose in making this text suitable as a tool for teaching. And, finally, I need once again to thank Bradley University for providing me with the resources to execute my scholarly endeavors. My chairman Tom Pucelik has been a true friend and colleague. His personal and professional support have made my years at Bradley rewarding ones.

I also wish to acknowledge my gratitude for having had so many fine teachers in the course of my life. Beginning with high school in East Grand Rapids, Michigan, both Bert Froysland and Jerry Norman taught me to think and to recognize the value of an examined life. I had the distinct privilege of receiving a spirited liberal arts education during my undergraduate years at Denison University. Don Tritt, Ron Santoni, Walter Eisenbeis, Jim Martin, and Lee Scott all contributed to the formation of the ideas that appear in this book. My graduate training at the University of Chicago was professionally engaging—in large part due to the influence of Martin Marty, Jerald Brauer, and Don Browning. And, finally, my years as a professor at

Bradley University have been enriched by a valued colleague, Kal Goldberg.

I would like to dedicate this book to my son, Bryan, in hope that both he and his generation will learn to care responsibly for their own and others' life cycles.

INTRODUCTION

Religion is a topic that continues to incite controversy and genuine intellectual debate. Seemingly simple questions provoke complex and divergent answers. Modern Americans, perhaps more than any other generation of human beings, wrestle with a variety of questions about the nature and meaning of religion: Is it important to be religious? Do humans have a need to be religious? If there is a need to be religious, does this need lead to human fulfillment or does it reflect a weakness which should be overcome if possible? If there isn't a fundamental tendency or need to be religious, is it possible that religions represent a premodern approach to life and that they ought to be replaced with more rational and scientific approaches to life's challenges?

This book seeks to examine such questions about the nature and value of religion from the perspective of modern psychology. That is, this book is concerned with how psychological understandings of human fulfillment enable us to understand the role religion plays in an individual's life. It is hoped that in doing so this book will accomplish at least two goals. First, this book aspires to use academic psychology to help locate the place of religion within the overall structure of a mature personality. We will, for example, look to developmental psychology for descriptions of the challenges and crises we

1

typically encounter over the course of our lives and then assess how religion affects our successful response to these challenges. The purpose of assessing religion in terms of its contribution to psychological well-being is to provide us with at least one means of distinguishing between those forms of religion that thwart and those that promote the widest range of human fulfillment. Second, by paying particular attention to the religious aspects of personal development, this book seeks to reexamine modern attitudes toward human nature. After all, the beliefs we hold about human nature shape our lives as individuals and profoundly influence the kind of society we create for ourselves. Our views concerning the limits and possibilities of human nature determine what we aspire to, what we seek to protect ourselves from, and what we find meaningful. They are, for this reason, also the stock of ideas that help us select values. Because our views of human nature identify the factors we believe influence personal fulfillment, they orient us in certain directions as we go about searching for meaning and happiness in our lives. It is thus of considerable importance that we occasionally reexamine our views about human nature and consider their suitability as guides to a maximum range of experience and enrichment. A major goal of this book, then, will be to ask whether the secularist style of thought associated with modern psychology is really commensurate with the full range of developmental challenges confronted across the life span or whether there are not, in fact, empirical grounds for viewing the life cycle in distinctively religious ways.

THE "PROBLEM" OF RELIGION
IN MODERN THOUGHT

The beginning of this century witnessed a remarkable shift in Americans' understanding of themselves and their place in the wider universe. The growth of both the natural and social sciences created a new intellectual climate which replaced the religious beliefs that had formerly constituted Americans' "official" ideas about the factors that control human destiny. The rapid advances made by science and technology altered the way in which educated men and women think about the laws and forces governing existence. Scientific method focuses upon observable laws of cause and effect; it has no room for the unprovable, the irrational, or even things that cannot in some way be quantified. The conceptual framework within which science identifies "causal factors" has thus systematically undermined the relevance of religious beliefs. The type of science that has been dominant throughout most of this century counts as "real" causes only those that are detectable by either our physical senses or technological extensions of those senses. As a consequence, the intellectual credibility of religion has been under continuous assault. It has become increasingly difficult to speak about religious influences or religious experience without giving the impression that one is referring to something that is less than fully real or that might be explained better by reducing it to explanations drawn from the conceptual categories of science.

Our modern social sciences, particularly psychology and sociology, were born of the progressivist spirit engendered by the natural sciences. Both psychology and sociology emerged as distinct intellectual disciplines by eschewing religious thought and boldly announcing that we can account for all the factors responsible for human well-being in terms of observable laws and forces. Psychology set itself to the task of describing "the good person" and "the good life" in ways that self-consciously avoided any religious considerations whatsoever. Likewise, sociology began to suggest ways in which we might build "the good society" through the application of empirically derived laws of human behavior. The cumulative effect of these two disciplines has been to edge religious interpretations of human nature out of modern intellectual thought.

It is helpful to review briefly the arguments against religion made by the two great intellectual giants of modern social science, Karl Marx (1818–1883) and Sigmund Freud (1856–1939). Both were convinced that the methods of social science demonstrated beyond doubt that religious thinking ranks among the most retrogressive forces in human life. Marx, an economic historian, observed how religion tends to divert our attention away from the real forces that determine the degree of happiness we will find in life. Marx argued that religion induces us to be concerned with intangible things such as a heaven or afterlife and in so doing discourages us from paying sufficient attention to the "real" economic causes of human happiness or misery. The illusory beliefs of religion thus stand in the way of practical efforts to improve the standard of living for the majority of people. True, religion comforts people in their misery by reassuring them that they will be compensated for their suffering when they reach heaven. But such comfort, according to Marx, works in the same pathetic way that opium does in giving suffering persons an illusory feeling of well-being even though it is inherently incapable of improving the conditions that actually caused this misery. Marx's message was clear. If we wish to better the condition of humankind and seek real happiness, we must first give up the kinds of illusory thinking fostered by religion and instead tackle our problems in a rational, technical manner.

Freud likewise viewed religion as a force that inherently and inevitably shackles the human spirit. The pioneer of modern psychotherapy, Freud observed how adults often revert to childish behaviors. When faced with difficult problems and crises, humans understandably feel weak and inadequate, much as they did as children. As a consequence, they find themselves yearning for a father figure and hoping that if they beg (i.e., pray) long enough he will help and protect them. The idea of a God or "Father who art in Heaven," then, is a symptom of the weakness of human nature. It is not that God created man out of his own image, but rather men and women who create the idea of god out of the image of a strong but caring and protecting father. Freud further reasoned that however understandable the psychological need for religion is, the fully mature adult must abandon it so as to face life with no false hopes, no illusions, no superstitions. Just as children should finally learn to give up their habitual begging in favor of a rational, problem-solving approach to life, so must the human race evolve past the stage of religious belief to enter an era of scientific rationality.

The overall effect of these trends in modern intellectual thought has been to shift American culture toward an increasingly secular outlook. The word secular here refers to the attitude of being indifferent to, or rejecting, religious considerations. Secularism thus indicates the shift toward humanism and away from theism. Whereas theism attributes all power and glory to god, humanism rejects the need to use religious concepts to speak about morals, values, or our highest potentials. Humanism maintains that men and women possess the capacity to improve their own lives through the use of reason alone and thus are in no way dependent upon either the guidance of scripture or the alleged power of prayers and rituals.

What makes these trends in our conceptions of human nature so significant is the often overlooked fact that the center of America's "official" ideas and attitudes long ago shifted from the church to the university. Universities are by definition committed to intellectual standards that favor concepts anchored in objective, publicly verified facts and observations. Hardheaded commitment to empirical facts will always carry more authority in a university setting than softhearted allegiance to religious faith. The consequence is that approximately three successive generations of college-educated Americans have come under the influence of conceptions of human nature that have no systematic place for religious aspects of, or influences upon, personality development.

THE LIMITS OF SCIENTIFIC
EMPIRICISM

By the 1960s, however, it became clear that the natural and social sciences were unlikely ever to give us the complete vision of human nature we had first expected from them. The more they developed, the more specialized they became. Science proceeds largely by narrowing rather than expanding the scope of issues it investigates. Science is, after all, the attempt to gain precise and verifiable knowledge of the objective world. The aims of the empirical method that science employs are shaped by the desire to derive public and definitive information. The empirical method allows this by selecting out of the totality of life's experiences only those "data" that are objectively discernible. Yet the subject matter suitable to scientific method is not life's whole. The entire range of humanity's moral and religious experience is omitted. As we shall be exploring in more detail in the following chapters, a recurring feature of human experience is the need to know not just what is, but what should be. Humans must make choices and decisions about the future; they must be able to envision and respond to social, interpersonal, and moral realities which are not "out there" in any simple or straightforward sense (e.g., the future, the "moral" environment). Thus even if the aims of scientific method were completely achieved, many vital human needs would remain unmet.

The problem facing all individuals is the problem of structuring their lives in ways that will best satisfy their needs and interests. Modern educated individuals, seeking objectively valid descriptions of our world, have appealed to the authority of experience and utilized the empirical methods of science as a guide to reality. They have hoped to understand better the forms of human behavior that will maximally contribute to their happiness and fulfillment by rejecting the unproven claims of religious scriptures and speculative philosophy. Yet the type of empiricism employed by science necessarily defines the environments we inhabit and to which we must adapt in ways that serve our personal and cultural needs poorly. Scientific empiricism cannot easily guide us in understanding those aspects of our experience that exist beyond the limits of objective measurement.

Over the past few decades a great deal of attention has been given to how our empirical methods of understanding reality might be expanded to include ranges of human experience that cannot be reduced to observable aspects of the outer environment. Much of this has come under the banner of concern for deriving "holistic" perspectives capable of accounting for human experience in all its diversity and complexity. The word holistic has been invoked to indicate a dissatisfaction with the reductionist tendencies of scientific empiricism. In particular, it expresses a concern to develop new ways of thinking about (1) the "environments" humans inhabit and (2) the types of interactions or "causal" influences that best enable us to adapt to these environments.

Contemporary Americans' interest in developing more encompassing models of human nature thus points directly to the shortcomings of modern science's (esp. psychology's) efforts to restrict its analysis of human experience to concepts of causality traditionally used in physics. We might, however, recognize at least four separate notions of causality which various cultures have utilized in their efforts to understand humanity's interaction with the universe: material causes (e.g., physiology, instincts, genetics); environmental causes (e.g., contingencies of environmental reinforcement, natural selection); mental/attitudinal causes (e.g., will power, suggestion, mood); and spiritual or "ultimate" causes (e.g., divine influence, spirit possession, achieving harmony with some metaphysical order of things). Modern psychology emerged as an academic discipline precisely owing to its determination to be a "psychology without a soul." By this modern psychologists have meant that the goal of scientific psychology is to describe human development exclusively in terms of causal processes which permit objective verification. Psychological explanations thus ordinarily invoke material (e.g., psychoanalytic discussions of the permutations that instinctual drives take as they encounter external resistance) and environmental (e.g., behaviorist emphasis on the environmental shaping of behavior) causes. Certainly many developmental theories utilize causal notions that refer to mental and attitudinal factors, but they do so somewhat defensively owing to the fact that they thereby equivocate their discipline's credentials as a "hard science."

The "problem" of religion in modern psychological thought can thus be thought of in terms of our general repudiation of definitions of reality and concepts of causality which would make religion relevant to our understanding of the laws and processes governing human existence. For example, even when advocates of what we have termed holistic thinking attempt to argue for the "spiritual" dimension of human well-being, they can at best utilize mental/attitudinal arguments. That is, they must fall back on such claims as "Religion imparts optimism" or "Faith in God helps alleviate stress which in turn aids the nervous and immune systems." What is lost here is any meaningful sense in which humans might indeed inhabit "worlds" that go beyond the subject-object sphere of rationality or whether our "adaptation" to these spheres might contribute to our overall course of development and well-being.

It is, as we shall see, possible to extend the empirical approach to the course of human development to include a consideration of what might meaningfully be described as the religious dimensions of human experience. By focusing upon the extent to which humanity's pursuit of happiness and fulfillment is contingent upon "adapting" to a spiritual environment beyond the limits of our physical and social worlds, we will gain a fresh look at the religious factors influencing the course of human development. It also promises to give us a theory of "natural religion"; that is, an account of the inherently and inescapably religious dimensions of human experience that is yet consistent with the methods and spirit of scientific inquiry.

RELIGION AND THE LIFE CYCLE

Religion is an elusive subject. For starters, there is little or no agreement concerning how the word "religion" should be defined or how it is best studied. Our starting point in this book must of necessity be an empirical one. That is, we are concerned with examining the ways in which religion develops and interacts amidst the full range of our motivations, aspirations, and psychological drives. Such an investigation, however, requires some working definition of religion such that "religious" aspects of experience can meaningfully be identified and distinguished from other modes of human functioning.

Academic approaches to the subject of religion tend to take one of two general approaches. The first emphasizes the formal properties or characteristics of religion that distinguish it from other subject matters and other aspects of human life. Formal definitions of religion typically seize upon some aspect of religious belief or experience and proceed to argue that this aspect represents "the" core of religion. For example, we might decide that belief in a god or gods is the distinguishing characteristic of religion and accordingly define religion in terms of worship practices or moral behavior associated with this kind of belief. The trouble with any such definition of religion is that many of the world's great religions do not have any conception of a god or goddess. Buddhism (especially in its Theravada form), for example, denies the existence of god. Confucianism, Taoism, and Shinto also lack the kinds of theistic belief that could make this a meaningful definition of religion. For this reason many scholars prefer instead to define the formal properties of religion in terms of its experiential rather than doctrinal characteristics. The clearest example of this type of formal definition of religion was offered by Rudolf Otto in his famous study of religion entitled *The Idea of the Holy*. Otto maintained that what distinguishes religion from other areas of life is the qualitatively distinct and unique feeling of the sacred or holy. Religion, according to Otto, emerges from the human apprehension of what he called "the wholly other." This "other" is experienced as awesome, numinous, fundamentally mysterious, and beyond our control; it subsequently evokes feelings of reverence, submission, dependence, rapture, and exaltation. But as with all formal definitions of religion, Otto's concept of the holy falls short of embracing the totality of what is commonly associated with religion. Only a small percentage of the world's population could honestly say that they have had such a life-altering experience. And, furthermore, this definition of religion is especially vulnerable to criticisms from sociologists and psychologists who might offer quite different interpretations of an individual's feeling of profound dependence or inner exaltation.

To avoid some of the problems associated with picking the formal properties of all religious beliefs and experiences, many scholars choose instead to define religion in functional terms. Functional definitions are less interested in what religion is than with what it does. For example, sociologists and anthropologists tend to define religion as a complex of beliefs and practices that facilitate social cohesion. Psychologists emphasize the role of religion in assisting individuals to overcome feelings of fear, loneliness, and guilt. Another common interpretation of the functional purpose of religion is the important task of giving life meaning and purpose. Insofar as humans are animals who ask questions about the origins and meaning of their lives, religion serves the indispensable function of orienting persons to a set of goals and values that can be experienced as meaningful and fulfilling. A major shortcoming of these kinds of definitions of religion, however, is that they seldom identify anything that could called distinctively religious. Nonreligious philosophies of life (e.g., capitalism, socialism, democracy) also give their adherents a sense of purpose and meaning. By reducing religion to its social and psychological functions there is a tendency to lose sight of anything that might be considered uniquely or distinctively religious.

The purpose of this book is to explore the nature and meaning of religion in a way that combines the formal and functional approaches. It will use a functional conception of religion in that it will be primarily concerned with examining the ways in which religion

originates and functions in common human experience. For this reason it will explicate religiosity primarily in terms of its psychological
functions. Yet to avoid the reduction of religion to aspects of human
experience that might better be explained in terms of physiological,
environmental, or even mental/attitudinal factors, we will confine
our description of the "religious" elements of human existence to
those experiences that disclose what theologian David Tracy describes as the limit dimension of the human condition.[1] The limit dimension of human experience refers to those situations in which
persons find themselves confronted with an ultimate limit or horizon to their experience. A "limit experience" is any moment of life
that forces us to acknowledge the limits or limitations of a strictly rational or empirical approach to life. They impart an awareness that
many of life's most profound challenges prompt us to look beyond
the resources and perspectives of the finite personality. As we shall
see, some limit experiences arise during periods of intellectual reflection and are thus of a more or less calm, even sedate character.
Others occur amidst highly emotional moments and thus partake of
the dramatic quality of either ecstasy or despair. Whichever the case,
what distinguishes a limit experience from other types of experience
is that it forces the individual to the recognition that reason, logic,
and worldly resources are alone incapable of adjusting us to some of
the most recurring themes in human experience.

Experiences that confront us with the "limit dimension" of human
existence can have either a negative (that is, arising in moments of
profound awareness of the limits or restrictions of finitude) or a positive (that is, arising in moments of seeming expansion beyond the ordinary limits of finitude) emotional tone. Limit experiences of the
"negative" variety arise in moments of grief, despair, or meaninglessness. They reveal in a poignant way that insofar as we view life solely
from the standpoint of this-worldly values we will derive no satisfac-
tory answers or solutions to our dilemma. Consider, for example,
such experiences of limit or limitation as awareness that we are going
to die in the near future, the death of a loved one, the loss of one or
more bodily functions, recognition of missed opportunities, or even
the struggle to answer tough moral and intellectual questions such as
Where did life come from? and Upon what power is life ultimately
dependent? In each and every one of these no successful resolution of

the problem at hand is possible within a strictly scientific or secularist perspective. That is, on strictly empirical grounds one might argue that there are any number of commonly recurring human experiences which seem to indicate that there are definite limits beyond which individuals cannot continue to grow or adequately address without first availing themselves of that which is in some way "beyond" the space-time physical world.

Limit experiences encountered as wholly "positive" reveal the existence and reality of that which lies beyond the limits of the physical universe. Mysticism, conversion experiences, participation in holy rituals or sacraments, and various altered states of consciousness all have a revelatory character insofar as they afford individuals a direct experience of a More or Beyond. Whereas negative limit experiences emerge amidst feelings of grief, confusion, or meaninglessness, positive limit experiences impart sensations of bliss, ecstasy, euphoria, and contentment. They impart to the conscious personality a firm conviction in the existence and even availability of a supersensible reality. The famed psychologist and philosopher William James defined religion in terms of an encounter with dimensions of reality that transcend the limits of the physical senses; religion arises in the encounter with an unseen or supersensible order of reality. The heart of religion, according to James, is the conviction that (1) the visible world is part of an unseen spiritual universe from which it draws its ultimate meaning or purpose, and (2) that union or harmonious relation with that higher universe is our true end as well as the key to achieving personal wholeness and well-being.[2]

Limit experiences, in other words, confront the individual with the awareness that there is some power or some higher level of consciousness which can resolve those disharmonies and feelings of incompleteness occurring at the "limits" of the human condition. They bring us to the conviction that *if* our lives can continue to be meaningful, *if* we can successfully handle the full gamut of mental, emotional, and moral challenges that typically confront humans over the course of their lives, and *if* we wish to interpret the relevance of a religious or mystical experience for our everyday life, *then* we must recognize that the "secret" to a life of maximum richness and fulfillment lies beyond the limits of the world known by science and beyond the limits of the self known by academic psychology.

This attempt to define religion in terms of limit experiences will not please those persons who are accustomed to thinking about religion in terms of belief in God, commitment to the Bible, or church attendance. After all, it "anchors" religion not in God but rather in a certain dimension of experiences common to individuals as they pursue their various courses of life. The importance of this approach, however, is that it more directly engages modern doubts about the nature, truth, or value of being religious. It enables us to take seriously the fact that the problem of doubt or unbelief in our era is rarely that of a debate between the believer and the unbeliever; it is instead the nagging voice of disbelief that each of us—even the self-identified believer—has about religion in an age committed to the intellectual styles of the natural and social sciences. The concept of the limit dimension of human experience allows us to pose the issue of religious faith in ways that embrace modern intellectual thought. More specifically, it permits us to view religious faith not as a set of unproven beliefs that we either do or do not hold but rather as a style of living influenced by the kinds of insights that occur just beyond the limits of either reason or sensory experience.

Examining the religious aspects of human development is particularly important as a first step toward answering such questions as Why be religious? and Isn't it possible to go through life both successfully and happily without any religious beliefs at all? These are questions our scientifically oriented age would seem to urge us answer in secular or nonreligious ways. But when the course of the human life cycle is viewed in its entirety, it becomes clear that there are numerous experiences or challenges that cannot be successfully dealt with within the limits of the individual's own intellectual and emotional resources. That is, even in modern scientific literature describing the typical stages of the human life cycle, we find recognition of the fact that many of the most important themes in human development are not reducible to science per se. At crucial stages in our course through life our happiness and fulfillment are dependent upon our ability to "adapt" not to the sensible world, but to the supersensible world; not to structures of physical and social reality but rather to that which lies just beyond the limits of the physical (i.e., the metaphysical). As we shall see, such experiences as midlife identity crises, moral struggles, and the need to embrace the aging process as a path toward continued personal development all lead individuals to the limit dimension of human experience. And for that reason they lay the foundations for a modern, coscientific view of the nature and relevance of religiousness in human existence.

ONE

RELIGION AND CHILDHOOD DEVELOPMENT

The task we have set ourselves is that of assessing the place of religion in the human life cycle. That is, we are attempting to examine the nature and functions of religion in terms of an individual's psychological development. It will be helpful, then, to begin by taking a look at commonly recurring experiences of the life cycle with an eye toward identifying those events or developmental stages that are most likely to disclose a "limit dimension" to human experience.

FULFILLMENT OVER THE LIFE CYCLE: ERIKSON'S EIGHT STAGES OF DEVELOPMENT

The writings of Sigmund Freud continue to be central to any understanding of the course of psychological development. We might estimate that about a third of all developmental theories build directly upon Freud's observations. Another third define their theoretical orientation by self-consciously rejecting, and offering alternatives to, the major tenets of Freud's theories. Even the third that more or less ignore Freud at least owe Freud the debt of having pioneered a view of human nature that emphasizes the significance of both infancy and childhood for determining the overall structure of personality development. Freud, a medical physician trained in an era greatly influenced by evolutionary biology, understandably emphasized the instinctual basis of human behavior. He assumed that individuals are more or less driven toward instinctual gratification and the release of pent-up instinctual pressure. Because the harsh realities of the natural and social environments do not always permit immediate instinctual release, individuals are forced to develop mental capacities that will enable them to restrain temporarily their instinctual urges and to find "acceptable" outlets. The stages of human development follow the pattern by which these restraining and coping skills are learned. Freud's vision of the optimal course of personality development was somewhat tragic. His interpretation of the asocial and destructive character of the bulk of our instinctual drives made it impossible for him to believe that persons would ever be fully or finally content. The mature adult life would at best be characterized by a calm, sober acceptance of the need to repress many of our biological urges for the sake of social stability.

We might briefly note how Freud's view of the origins and function of religion in human life parallel his overall developmental theory. Freud interpreted religion in two principal ways. First, he viewed religion as a form of immature thinking; it represents an unwillingness to accept the harsh realities of existence. As we mentioned in the Introduction, Freud believed that religion represents a childlike orientation to the world in which our wishes and desires dominate our perception of reality. The vulnerability of the human condition in the face of such terrifying realities as disease, natural disasters, or the imminence of death causes us to yearn for safety and protection. Just as a child responds to insecurity by turning to his or her parent, so too do adults often begin to wish for a father figure to deliver them from evil and provide them with the basic necessities of life. Such religious belief, however, is built upon superstition and irrational wishes and thus stands in the way of the development of a strong, rational outlook on life.

The second of Freud's perspectives on religion has to do with the cultural function of religion in getting us to repress our sexual and asocial instinctual urges and instead to conform to conventional ethical standards. The developmental need to suppress selfish desires and acquire rational self-control comes to a head in what Freud termed the Oedipal crisis, in which a young boy must renounce his sexual lust for his mother and accept the authority and external inhibitions represented by his father. Freud believed that religion provides cultural support and sanction for this process. The concept of God is a powerful reinforcement for persons' willingness to recognize and obey a "higher" power of father figure beyond themselves. In short, religion serves the socially necessary function of inducing individuals to renounce their asocial desires and to abide by the community's moral standards.

Freud's contributions to the study of personality development have been progressively elaborated, revised, and in many cases even abandoned over the last several decades. Surprisingly, however, few psychologists have sought to supplement or refine his essentially negative view of the role of religion in the course of human development. The reason for this is undoubtedly academic psychology's overwhelming commitment to theories that emphasize material (e.g., genetic endowment, instinct) and environmental (e.g., contingencies of reinforcement) causes of behavior. Hence most psychological theories are similar to Freud's at least to the extent that they share his basic view that religion is not a "real" factor in human development.

Because the major goal of this book is to offer an empirically based understanding of the religious dimensions of human fulfillment across the life cycle, it requires a model of psychological development that incorporates mental/attitudinal causes and is at least neutral toward the phenomenological features of humanity's experiences of an "ultimate" order or power of life. The well-known writings of Erik Erikson will guide us in this task. Although rooted in Freud's psychoanalytic tradition, Erikson's theories open up sufficiently broader perspectives on the nature of selfhood that a more perceptive vision of the religious aspects of life is possible. It is helpful to note that Erikson's theories differ from Freud's in three major ways. First, he rejects Freud's assumption that instinctual drives constitute the primary or basic order of human functioning. Whereas Freud spoke of human behavior as being "driven" by instinctual urges, Erikson puts more emphasis on the role of the social environment in stimulating us to action. For Erikson, such environmental influences as siblings, peers, parents, and various historical and cultural institutions all play a primary role in eliciting our adaptive behaviors. Second, Erikson places greater emphasis on the conscious personality or ego. In contrast to Freud's characterization of the ego as a relatively weak agent at the mercy of both instinctual demands and social inhibitions, Erikson accredits the ego with the capacity to regulate the individual's relationships with the environment in ways that not only achieve personal wholeness but make positive contributions to the fulfillment of others as well. The importance of this is that Erikson thereby gives mental/attitudinal (what Aristotle called "final") causes as great, or greater, a role in determining our well-being as either material or environmental factors. It might also be noted that although Erikson never deviates from a strictly psychological accounting of human experience and behavior, his studies of religious individuals such as Gandhi and Luther sensitized him to the empirical data of the life-enhancing qualities of humanity's efforts to approach the ultimate limits or horizons of the sensible universe. Third, Erikson is more optimistic than Freud in that he continuously points out developmental opportunities conducive to growth. His psychology is so structured as to accord itself with those developmental processes that lead to growth and the differentiation of potentials rather than with the symptoms that appear when these processes have been thwarted.

According to Erikson, human development proceeds according to something like a timetable or schedule. This developmental schedule consists of eight successive stages. Erikson notes that development is an evolutionary process based upon a sequence of biological, psychological, and social events. Life is a continual process. It consists of constant motion in which an individual never really "has" a personality, but continuously develops and redevelops his or her sense of individual identity.

Erikson notes that each of the eight stages presents individuals with a new developmental challenge. If individuals are to grow and develop in a strong and creative way they must successfully meet this challenge, resolve it, and integrate what it has taught them into their ongoing sense of identity. Sometimes Erikson refers to these challenges as developmental "tasks" which successively confront us over the course of the life span and require us to develop new methods for relating to, and interacting with, our social environments. At other times he refers to them as "crises" to indicate situations that have come to the crucial moment where an outcome or direction—whether for good or for bad—is inevitably taking shape. Each stage thus presents individuals with a task or challenge that must be successfully resolved before they can move forward in their psychological development.

In Erikson's view, we never master any developmental task or crisis by ourselves. The perspective of the life cycle permits him to see how fully each and every life interlocks with others. At every stage of our development we simultaneously benefit from, and contribute to, the lives of others. There is no such thing as a self-made person—individuals are not islands unto themselves. Like cogwheels that only move forward by meshing or interconnecting with others, we require other people (our parents when we are young, friends during our teen-age years, a lover during our young adulthood, our children during our parenting years, and God—however conceived—as we face the final crisis of the life cycle). However, just as individuals are incapable of activating personal growth solely on their own, no one can force a person to grow if he or she does not decide to grow. Every step we take is really one of mutual cooperation in the enterprise of life. Erikson calls this *mutual activation.* By this he means that we grow as we help others. In the act of giving of yourself to another, you simultaneously occasion growth within yourself. For example, a mother tirelessly gives of herself to her young child without any consideration of her own needs; but paradoxically, in the process she becomes fulfilled as a woman and mother. The same is true for two people in love. Only when you finally escape self-centeredness and truly care for another will you ever activate real love in yourself. You grow and fulfill yourself as you help others grow and become fulfilled. In Erikson's words, human growth "depends from stage to stage upon a network of mutual influences within which the person actuates others even as he is actuated, and within which the person is inspired with active properties even as he inspires others."[1]

Four of the eight stages that Erikson believes capture the essential critical tasks or challenges of the life cycle pertain to childhood. It is important to note that no claim is being made that Erikson's stage approach to the human life cycle has anything in the way of universal validity or applicability. It reveals, for example, a distinctively Western outlook and tends to make male, rather than female, patterns of development normative.[2] The former is less troublesome for our purposes than the latter in that our inquiry into the nature and value of religion is intended to respond to the kinds of difficulties that modern, educated individuals in the Western world often have in assessing the role of religion in personal life. The eight virtues or personality strengths Erikson observes in the course of optimal psychological development provide just such an arena in which to argue over the relative strengths and weaknesses of religion in promoting human fulfillment. We must, however, be wary of the masculine gender bias ubiquitous in academic psychology and recognize that Erikson's theories will have distinct limitations in characterizing female developmental patterns. Perhaps the most important of these is Erikson's tendency to make "optimal" development always appear as part of individuals' attempts to become increasingly separate or detached from those around them. Carol Gilligan has pointed out that "women depict ongoing attachment as the path that leads to maturity" and that "women replace the bias of men toward separation with a representation of the interdependence of self and other, both in love and in work."[3] If we remain wary of possible gender differences such as those Gilligan suggests, Erikson is still a helpful point from which to begin our survey of the developmental "prerequisites" of personal happiness and fulfillment. We turn now to his description of the psychological tasks or challenges confronted in our early years.

Stage 1
Approximate Age: The Newborn
Acquiring a Sense of Basic Trust
(while overcoming a sense of
basic mistrust)
A Realization of Hope

Like most psychologists, Erikson believes that the earliest years of our lives are very crucial in setting the basic foundations of our personality. Erikson believes that infancy presents the developmental task or challenge of securing a basic trust in life, of being able to experience life as something that can and should be trusted rather than feared as a chaotic, hostile place. The critical theme in this first developmental phase, then, is avoiding mistrust of life and instead acquiring hope.

The degree to which infants are able to trust the world (themselves and other people) depends mostly on the quality of care they receive from the mother. The infant whose needs are met promptly, whose discomforts are quickly removed, who is cuddled, fondled, played with, and talked to, develops a sense that the world is a safe place to be and that people are dependable and helpful. If, on the other hand, the care is inconsistent and inadequate, the young infant never develops a truly trusting and positive attitude toward the world and other people.

A child can develop a basic sense of trust in life only if he or she enjoys an overall feeling of physical comfort and has a minimum of fear and frustration. If these are provided, this trust will extend to new experiences. In contrast, a sense of mistrust leads to anxiety and apprehensiveness. A fundamental trust in life, Erikson notes, is absolutely indispensable to continued psychological growth and the ability to readily and willingly seek out new experiences.

It is important to realize that although the crisis surrounding the development of trust or mistrust is the major developmental task of the first year of life, it is never resolved once and for all. More than any theme of the other eight stages of the life cycle, the theme of acquiring trust and avoiding mistrust recurs again and again as we progress through life. For example, a twenty-year-old may have an essentially trustful attitude toward life but, following the death of a parent or a breakup with a boyfriend or girlfriend, come to fear life as threatening or hurtful. Conversely, an individual who has never found life responsive to his or her inner needs may through a newfound love or a religious experience suddenly discover a basic trust in life.

Erikson has noted that religion is the major means by which individuals either acquire, or reaffirm, their basic trust in life. The issue of trust is an essentially religious one because what is at stake here is not the amount of information we have about this or that aspect of life. The whole of reality, not its isolated parts, is in question. It is a matter of the origins, meaning, and purpose of the entire universe. And this is not a scientific issue but rather an existential judgment concerning that which lies beyond the limits of human observation; it invokes faith—or lack of faith—in the presence and activity of that which lies beyond the physical appearance of life and imbues it with its funda-mental character. And, as Erikson observes, one of the major psycho-logical functions of religious beliefs and rituals is to reassure individuals of the essential goodness of creation. Erikson says that if we successfully resolve the crisis of trust versus mistrust we acquire hope. Hope is the belief that our wishes can be obtained in spite of difficulties. Hope is the virtue that makes faith possible, and adult faith in turn nourishes hope and inspires us to care for others.

Stage 2
Age: Early Childhood, 2–4
Acquiring a Sense of Autonomy
(while combating a sense of shame and doubt)
A Realization of Will

As infants gain trust in their mother and world, they start to dis-cover their own capacity to act and cause effects in their environ-ment. They begin to assert a degree of autonomy; they begin to realize their capacity to will. The crisis that develops is occasioned by opposing desires to maintain dependence upon one's parents and to exercise this growing autonomy. Dependency upon parents is cou-pled with the warmth, love, and unqualified approval that are be-stowed upon helpless infants. As the child begins to develop, it loses this attention and care and subsequently begins to doubt whether this exertion of individuality and autonomy is a worthwhile en-deavor. When coupled with his or her poorly developed abilities to coordinate body movements, communicate, and so forth, this sense of doubt often becomes accompanied by shame as well.

This is a stage in which parental care is a crucial factor. Parents must help their children balance self-initiated actions with the restraints imposed upon them by society. Parents must be careful to encourage active play and experimentation while simultaneously putting a limit on their actions so that they will not hurt themselves or become ut-terly undisciplined. Punishment begins here. Punishment is neces-sary in putting a control on the individual's growing autonomy, but it must not cause doubt and shame. The type of behavior parents per-mit and the way in which they exert control over the child will have a direct bearing upon his or her attitude toward ideals, authority, and social organizations later in life. The point here is that the type of child training determines an individual's sense of authority—how much authority does he or she have as an individual and how much does society have? Are individual actions valuable or are they going to be punished?

Religious beliefs both directly and indirectly seek to guide individuals toward some resolution of this developmental challenge. For instance, doctrines concerning the nature and/or limitations of human free will provide broad clues concerning a religious community's understanding of the proper balance between individual autonomy and group controls. It must be remembered, however, that religious doctrines are principally directed toward adults rather than children. It is quite possible that many religious doctrines emphasizing the dangers of humanity's attempts to be self-directing rather than passively obedient to God's will reflect a religious community's attempts to put constraints on adolescent and adult tendencies toward asocial conduct. Unfortunately, the kind of cultural ethos engendered by such doctrines could potentially have a debilitating impact upon those individuals who have not yet developed a strong sense of personal autonomy and are thus quite vulnerable to feelings of shame and doubt.

The strength of virtue hopefully acquired in this stage is that of will. Will is the unbroken determination to exercise free choice as well as self-restraint, in spite of unavoidable moments of shame and doubt.

Stage 3
Approximate Age: 4–5
Acquiring a Sense of Initiative and
Overcoming a Sense of Guilt.
A Realization of Purpose

By the fourth or fifth year a child has matured to the point where he or she is ready to express the urge to live in an exuberant, unharnessed way. Whether children will emerge from this stage with their sense of initiative far outbalancing their sense of guilt depends to a considerable extent upon how parents respond to their self-initiated activities. Children who are given much freedom and opportunity to initiate motor play such as running, wrestling, sports, or general play around the home will have their sense of initiative reinforced. Initiative is also reinforced when parents answer their children's questions (intellectual initiative). On the other hand, if children are made to feel that their actions are upsetting to the parent or that their questions are a nuisance then they will invariably feel uneasy and even guilty about their own desires and actions. Such guilt may well persist through later life stages leaving the individual without a sense of confidence or assertiveness.

In much the same way that religious beliefs attempt to reinforce particular resolutions of the developmental challenge concerning autonomy, so too do they guide individuals toward certain ways of balancing tendencies toward either a sense of initiative or guilt. Doctrines concerning a sense of "vocation," "mission," or "stewardship" all seek to align individual initiative with a community's religious and ethical values. Conversely, notions concerning innate depravity or original sin induce a sense of uneasiness and guilt about one's impulses toward self-determined activity. Again, it might be pointed out that developmental psychology suggests that the kinds of lessons or guidance appropriate to one stage or aspect of our personal growth might be quite inappropriate to persons who have yet to secure permanently a successful resolution of an "earlier" stage. And thus just as certain religious doctrines might help an individual forge a cohesive and essentially positive sense of self, it is also possible that they could have permanently debilitating effects upon psychological development.

The personality virtue that, hopefully, emerges from early experiences with self-generated initiative is that of purpose. Purpose is the courage to envisage and pursue valued goals without being inhibited by fear of punishment or guilt.

Stage 4
Approximate Age: 6–11
Acquiring a Sense of Industry
(and fending off a sense of inferiority)
A Realization of Competence

The child's developing skills bring the potential for interaction with ever-widening social environments. This is the point at which the environment expands to include others of his or her own age. The child's energies now become committed to working on social prob-

lems or adjusting to the rules that govern friendships. During this period peers assume a position equal to that of adults. Peers are needed
as resources for building one's own self-esteem and earliest formulations of identity. And consequently the school comes to compete
with the family as the locus of personality development.

During these years a child becomes concerned with self-
improvement and acquiring the ability to interact successfully with
both objects and other people. The child's drive to succeed includes
an awareness of the possibility or threat of failure. This underlying
fear impels young children to work harder to succeed and avoid feelings of mediocrity. It is crucially important here to avoid developing a
sense of inferiority so that the child will possess the self-assurance to
move confidently forward in life.

Acquiring a sense of industry gives rise to the virtue or strength of
competence. Competence is the free exercise of intelligence and
physical skills to complete tasks unimpaired by feelings of inferiority.

This is also a stage when many children begin religious education,
either in Sunday schools or in the home through the reading of Bible
stories, and so forth. We might already begin to ask ourselves about
the effect of religious teachings on the development of such personality attributes as will, purpose, or competence. What values are
being transmitted here, what do they teach the child, and do they
accelerate—or impede—the acquisition of skills that will help the
developing individual adjust to the challenges of life?

STAGES AND STAGE TRANSITION

The four stages Erikson discerns in childhood development reflect
the individual's acquisition of increasingly differentiated adaptive
strengths. Stages refer to the emergence of an equilibrium or relative
balance between individuals' skills for interacting with the environment and the demands the environment places upon them. What
must be kept in mind, however, is that most of our lives are spent "between" rather than "in" stages. Continuous physiological maturation and ever-shifting environmental demands disrupt any previous
equilibrium. Life has more to do with the transitions and transformations that challenges elicit than it does with resting places.

Stage transitions follow a fairly distinct pattern.[4] The first phase of transition begins when an earlier or less differentiated condition is disrupted either by physiological maturation or changing environmental demands. The pressure exerted by these internal or external changes forces the individual's acquisition of a more differentiated form of relating to the world such that more complex situations can be managed successfully. Older patterns of relating to the world are now too narrow and idiosyncratic to be of use. The disruption of equilibrium initiates the second phase of transition during which the individual must develop any number of new relational skills. We might call this the phase of adding new, specialized skills to one's mental, emotional, and behavioral repertoires. Thus, for example, the young child going off to school for the first time must go through a somewhat painful trial-and-error period in which she or he experiments with facial expressions, play behaviors, greeting gestures, and so forth, in order to relate successfully with the teacher, peers, and new physical surroundings.

Transitions also elicit a third phase in which we learn to integrate our newly acquired skills. In this phase we develop a new, more differentiated pattern of psychological or personality organization. The integration of these learned skills into an organized whole permits the emergence of overall or basic personality strengths such as trust, autonomy, initiative, and industry. Finally, because this new pattern of interaction is more efficient and rewarding it simultaneously produces the reinforcement necessary to establish itself as an integral part of the personality. The newly acquired virtues or strengths "prove themselves" through their ability to enhance and enlarge the individual's range of satisfaction.

This transitional process, as we shall see, continues throughout life. And, importantly, as the life cycle progresses the triggering experience of human development and transformation is increasingly likely to come in the form of a limit experience.

CHILDREN AND THE IDEA OF GOD

Over the past twenty years a new school or branch of psychoanalytic thought known as object relations theory has emerged. Object relations theory (as well as its cousin movement known as self psychology) is based on Freud's insights concerning the lasting psychological influence of early relationships with others. What Freud had discovered is the fact that our earliest experiences of something outside or beyond ourselves are initially of objects (e.g., the mother's eyes, breasts, hands) and only secondly of persons. These early environmental objects, moreover, leave images or imagos which have lasting influences on our perception of reality. Theorists such as Melanie Klein, Otto Kernberg, D. W. Winnicott, and Heinz Kohut have contributed a great deal of additional support for this theory, yet have differed from Freud to the extent that (1) they are more interested in the early development of a cohesive sense of selfhood (prior to the Oedipal struggle which dominated Freud's interests), and (2) they give a far greater role to nonrational mental activities such as fantasy and imagination in guiding our adaptive processes.

According to the object relations theorists, the principal "challenge" of our first two years of life—a challenge that, incidentally, will continue throughout life—is that of gradually separating our self-image from the image of the nurturing parent. Beginning with these earliest encounters with the world, humans are caught between two compelling and conflicting psychological needs that are rooted in the human condition as such. On the one hand, we are driven by the need to have a prized, cohesive sense of self; we have the need to stand out, be separate, and express individuality. On the other hand, we have an equally compelling need for merger, for community, for uniting with an idealized imago or parent from which we will receive security and, via our attachment to that valued object, receive a sense of meaningfulness. Throughout the entire course of life we need to address and balance the conflicting needs for a sense of autonomy and for alliance with a "higher" power.

Object relations theory sheds a great deal of light on the origin and continued functions of the concept of God in our psychological system.[5] The beginning of a God representation would appear to be in infancy when the child develops the earliest capacities for play and imagination. The child does this largely through acts of fantasy or imagination in which he or she views the world in ways that blur the sharp distinction adults make between internal and external reality and instead creates a kind of intermediate area or space that offers a safe transition between these two realms and in so doing unites them. Winnicott, for example, calls this the capacity to form relations with a "transitional object" such as a doll, teddy bear, or imaginary friend; this transitional object permits safe venturing out of the vulnerable internal realm to learn to interact with, and make contributions to, an independent reality. As Winnicott notes, this transitional zone of fantasy and play continues throughout life and makes possible our engagement with the "arts and to religion and to imaginative living and to creative scientific work."[6]

Between the ages of two and five a child has generally established this capacity to create transitional space and then enters another critical phase of psychological development. About this time his or her transitional space becomes alive with heroes, villains, imaginary friends, and fairy-tale characters. And, as Ana-Marie Rizzuto has shown,

> Together with this colorful crowd of characters, and amidst intense phallic, vaginal preoccupations, fantasies, wishes and fears, God arrives. It first may seem one more in the procession. Soon, however, God acquires a special and superior status on account of multiple socio-cultural, religious, ritualistic, familiar and—not least—epigenetic phenomena.[7]

The mental image of God, as with these other friends and companions, helps buoy the child's sense of self as he or she must necessarily become more separated and distanced from the nurturing parent. The relationship a child establishes with these transitional objects helps her or him tolerate feelings of inadequacy, shame, and frustration. And, as other imaginary objects gradually lose their power to sustain a realistic experience of being related to a valued "higher power," the concept of God continues to maintain what Rizzuto calls its "superior status." Unlike other transitional objects, God is a symbol-concept which represents the entire culture's values, strivings, aspirations, and defenses. Thus the symbol of God shapes an ontological reality, not only for its believers, but for all those who live within its symbolic reach.[8] The concept of God, then, is not just a projection of the human father as Freud suggested. It emerges as a type of collective representation or gestalt of any number of powerful factors: the characteristics of the mother and the father, the dynamics of the twofold need to merge with a higher power and yet simultaneously to experience oneself as autonomous, and the general social, historical, and religious background of the family. The concept of God, according to object relations theory,

> is *not* an illusion. It is an integral part of being human, truly human in our capacity to create nonvisible but meaningful realities capable of containing our potential for imaginative expansion beyond the boundaries of our senses.[9]

The fundamental point being made here is that the concept of God emerges and takes root very early in our psychological development. The fact that it takes shape amidst images drawn both from early infancy and from one's sociohistorical setting and utilizes these images through fantasy and imagination does not in any way deprecate either the truth or meaning of this symbol-concept. Quite the contrary. The image of God emerges amidst the disequilibrium initiated by the gradual separation from the nurturing parent. It heals and brings vitality to the self by drawing it out into relationship with the world in ways that support its basic ontological need for autonomy and for relationship with a higher or ultimately meaningful "other." And thus it begins to prove itself and make possible for life the potential for imaginative expansion beyond the boundaries of our senses.

RELIGION AND PRIMARY SOCIALIZATION

In addition to its role in enhancing our psychological capacity for creative and imaginative involvement with the world, religion is also a vehicle for the overall socialization process. Religious thinking and behavior develop part and parcel with our overall assimilation into the larger familial, social, and cultural patterns of life. The two primary avenues of this learning process are *imitation* and *identification*. Children begin imitating their parents and older siblings at a very early age. Play, speech, eating at the table, and waving bye-bye all begin as imitated behaviors. Religious behaviors, too, begin in this fashion. Children learn to fold their hands and bow their heads in prayer long before they grasp the meaning of these gestures. The words of a prayer have no more significance to a child than those of a favorite bedtime story. In either case, what is most important to the child is that familiar words be precisely and routinely repeated. The influential modern psychologist Gordon Allport related an account of a young boy who said bedtime prayers every night in front of a religious picture.[10] One night the picture wasn't available, so the boy instead located a cover of *The Saturday Evening Post* and, thoroughly satisfied, resumed his prayers as usual. As this incident illustrates, religion for children largely consists of imitated behaviors. They are repeated again and again as part of the process of learning to conform to the family's way of life. Children's performance of religious behaviors thus has little or no meaning beyond its significance as a form of social training. By repeating the ritual behaviors and memorizing the mythic beliefs of their families and tribes, young children become incorporated into the patterns of their culture.

The other major avenue of early socialization is the process whereby children learn to identify with significant persons in their environment. Identification with the same-sex parent or older brothers and sisters hastens a child's acquisition of those stereotyped behaviors and attitudes that the child soon learns that society expects. The identification process gradually extends to ever wider social roles. Children often learn to identify with the company or corporation their parents work for and view rival companies as in some way "bad." They eventually learn to identify with their grade school, city, state, and nation, and simultaneously acquire the values and attitudes they assume New Yorkers, Texans, or Americans stand for. The author once gave a lecture entitled "What is a Protestant?" to a seventh-grade class. At the end of the lecture one attentive young boy raised his hand and asked me if I could explain what a Presbyterian was. Just before beginning a lengthy discussion of the Westminster Confession and John Knox's role in the early Protestant movement, I realized that I had best pause and first ask the boy why he wanted to know about Presbyterians. He replied, "My parents told me that we're Presbyterians and even though we don't go to church, I want to know what religious doctrines I believe in."

This little story reveals a great deal about the child's acquisition of religious beliefs. The dual processes of imitation and identification commit the child to acquiring the beliefs and attitudes of his or her parents. In many respects a child unconsciously agrees to believe in the absolute truth of religious doctrines before he or she even knows what these doctrines are. Because they identify you as belonging to the in-group of family and friends, they symbolize commitment to all that is safe, familiar, good, and true. There is, moreover, an interesting implication to the fact that a child's early religious beliefs are acquired as a byproduct of identifying with parents and other significant adults. It would appear that the sincerity of the parents would be a crucial factor in the child's perception of the attitude to take toward religious ideas and practices. Thus, those parents who take their children to church even though they do not personally believe in religion may unwittingly transmit the very superficiality or indifference they assumed they were guarding against.

Sunday school attendance, family Bible reading, summer Bible camps, and the diffuse dissemination of religious beliefs through television shows, and so on, are all agents of the socializing process. They, as with other socializing agents such as schools or scouting organizations, have a significant impact on the individual's resolution of the developmental crises of will, purpose, and competence. No overall assessment of the influence that religion has in terms of either promoting or hindering these personality virtues can be made. Certainly many churches so emphasize humanity's innate depravity and dependence upon God as to thwart an individual's sense of initiative and self-determination. On the other hand, the well-known maxim that "God helps those who help themselves" surely encourages the cultivation of personal initiative while yet doing so in a way that would minimize unlimited selfishness or insensitivity to others. And, too, such allied virtues as responsibility, conscientiousness, and courtesy are traditionally fostered in religious settings.

What should be understood here is the fact that churches exert considerable influence upon the course of personality development. Of course this is only minimally the case for those whose families have no formal religious commitments. And it is is also questionable whether religion has any particular relevance to the major developmental themes of childhood insofar as they pertain mostly to a process of learning to conform to the most immediate elements of the natural and social environments. But indeed, insofar as religion becomes embodied in doctrines and institutions, it certainly gives patterns and direction to a developing individual's life.

THE SECOND-HAND QUALITY OF
CHILDHOOD BELIEF

In his classic study of religion, *The Varieties of Religious Experience,* Williams James made a distinction between what he called firsthand and secondhand religious faith.[11] The former refers to the individual in whom religion has become a living reality and who adheres to religious convictions on the basis of experiential evidence. The latter, secondhand faith, refers to the individual who has been socialized into a set of religious beliefs and practices but has not personally experienced the realities to which they attest. Secondhand religious faith consists of memorized doctrines and role behaviors which are adhered to more out of dull habit than life-enhancing zest.

It should be obvious that the religiosity of late childhood or early adolescence is almost inherently of the secondhand variety. This is so principally because few of the challenges that draw children forth to interact with their world have a distinctly "limit" character to them. We have, of course, already noted how such developmental issues as the formation of basic trust and the capacity to create or envision transitional space have ontological in addition to strictly psychological dimensions. Which is to say that childhood faith is an active process of invention and construction whereby the world is engaged in complex and meaning-constructing ways. The fact that these active modes of world-construction are significantly influenced by the symbols, gestures, and attitudes of those closest to them does not in any way detract from the fresh, imaginative character of a child's religious engagement of reality. We must, nonetheless, also assess childhood religiosity from the standpoint of developmental challenges which will be faced as adolescence and adulthood grow nearer. Among these challenges will be the need to integrate diverse intellectual means for seeking truth and the need to take responsibility for one's own cognitive commitments. It is from this perspective that we can see the extent to which the religion of children is less an active part of their own effort to engage life as it is a socialization phase of acquiring the set of stories, morals, and ideas being handed down to them from an older generation. Their ability to grasp and interpret these religious beliefs is, of course, restricted by their overall cognitive and emotional development. We will return to examine the process whereby religious beliefs become ever more cognitively sophisticated at the end of the next chapter. For now it is sufficient that we briefly recognize the psychological characteristics typically associated with children's religious beliefs.

The secondhand nature of childhood religiosity can, according to psychologist Walter Houston Clark, be characterized as (1) accepted on authority, (2) anthropomorphic, (3) concrete and literal, (4) egocentric, (5) imitative, and (6) unreflective.[12] A religious faith that has not yet undergone the metamorphosis into maturity is, according to Clark, ordinarily based upon external authority rather than personal experience or reasoned arguments. Secondhand religious faith is accepted on the authority of parents, sacred texts, or ordained clergy; its validity is thus unquestioned and exempt from critical investigation. Because religious faith of this sort is based largely on the stories and doctrines encountered in Scriptures and Sunday school classes, it is thus characterized by a kind of uncritical anthropomorphism. That is to say, the human literary or mythological imagination tends to create God in our own image. Everyday religious language pictures God along the lines of a superior human being. We commonly refer to God with words such as "Omnipotent Father," "King," "Ruler," and so forth. Many children gradually assimilate a very humanlike image of God and tend to envision the divine as a kind of thinner Santa Claus or a Superman-like figure with a big G on his chest.[13] Religious beliefs acquired from others on no other basis than conformity also tend to be excessively concrete and literal. Young children, of course, are not yet capable of higher and more complex thinking processes. For this reason religious stories and instruction traditionally have a vividly literal dimension to them. And, until such time as the individual begins to engage in abstract speculation concerning the riddle of existence or encounters ideas that necessitate a critical reexamination of religious belief, he or she will tend to view religious beliefs and practices very literally (not unlike this author who as a youngster asked his mother out loud during a Christian communion service what part of Jesus' body she had—a leg, breast, or thigh?).

According to Clark, the secondhand religious faith common in childhood is largely egocentric. Belief in a god is tied up with self-interest. Prayers to God differ little from wish lists sent to Santa Claus; that is, they request personal favors in exchange for assurances that we will be nice little boys and girls. At this stage of development religion is, as we have already seen, largely imitative. Religious beliefs are adhered to and religious rituals performed as though uniformity is a value in and of itself. Religion, when adopted secondhand, has the look and feel of a one-size-fits-all commodity. Much like a product bought ready made, it has yet to be altered in any way to adapt it better into the individual's overall pattern of life. Related to the imitative character of secondhand religion is what Clark calls its unreflective nature. By this he means that the individual has to this point not as yet confronted doubts and ambiguities concerning his or her religious faith. Unreflective faith maintains mental barriers between religion and all other areas of life so as to minimize any potential conflict in what professes to be true. This is, of course, ordinarily the case for children who are largely ignorant of the discrepancy between commitment to the scientific method of reasoning and unquestioning faith in scriptures. Unreflective faith avoids confronting other possible discrepancies such as the nagging issue of why there can be evil in the world if God is truly all-powerful and all-good and the obvious problem of maintaining confidence in the existence of "one, true" faith in the face of numerous religious traditions espoused by sincere, intelligent individuals, each of whom is equally convinced of adhering to the "best" religion. Whatever else one might say about unreflective faith, it has certainly not yet become integrated into the individual's total approach to life.

As childhood gives way to adolescence and young adulthood, pressures come to bear upon a religious faith acquired from without on the basis of parental authority. The late teens and twenties afford individuals their first opportunities to make the somewhat turbulent transition from a secondhand to a firsthand religious faith.

TWO

BELIEF AND IDENTITY
FORMATION

The late teens and early twenties witness a profound transformation in our primary mode of responding to the world. During this pivotal period in the life cycle, we shift from the status of being essentially dependent upon adults to becoming adults ourselves. Along with this transition comes the acquisition of ever-increasing ranges of autonomy and self-determination, as well as the responsibilities that come with them.

One of the most important characteristics of this stage of life is the maturation of our cognitive skills to include the capacity for abstract thought. As the noted cognitive psychologist Jean Piaget has demonstrated, mental development proceeds through a series of successive stages. Beginning with the simplest reflex behaviors in infants, mental skills develop gradually as the individual learns to incorporate ever-widening ranges of life into his or her repertoire of adaptive behaviors. By the teen-age years, we become capable for the first time of representative or abstract thought. The capacity for abstract thought makes it possible for us to construct hypothetical responses to any given situation. We learn to imagine acting in a wide variety of ways, being a wide variety of persons. It is, of course, precisely this capacity for abstract and hypothetical reasoning that makes the issue of identity formation a developmental task or crisis. Questions such

as, Who am I? Who should I become? and What do I believe in? no
longer have simple answers. Each can now be approached from any
number of angles and numerous possibilities can be entertained.
What is more, the moral and religious beliefs formerly acquired secondhand in a rather unquestioning way can now be reexamined from
other points of view. Individuals begin to ask themselves whether social conditioning is alone responsible for their religious beliefs. If
they had been born in the family down the block, let alone in another
country, would they now believe in entirely different sets of "absolute" truths? They begin to detect relativity in ideas formerly assumed to be absolute, hypocrisy amidst what before was thought to
be utter sincerity, logical contradictions among what were earlier
thought to be compatible methods for ascertaining what is true,
right, or good.

The onset of critical thinking abilities orients youth to the intellectual or doctrinal aspects of religion. Young persons are particularly
conscious of the need to reexamine the beliefs and values that have
been handed to them by adult authorities. Peer influence and opinion now supersede parental control. For some, this might mean intensified commitment to a church and its doctrines. This is
especially the case where a sufficient number of one's peers have intellectually and socially identified themselves with the church. For
most persons, however, this is a period of indifference to, or even out-
right rebellion against, the seemingly coercive authority associated
with parents and other adult authorities. Studies have shown, in fact,
that youth is the least religious period in an individual's life insofar
as religion is identified as expressed concern with church doctrines
and institutions.[1] Youth are instead far more concerned with their
immediate social relationships, recreation, "getting to the top," financial security, and peer respect. In other words, youth is too preoccupied with adapting to the interpersonal, educational, and socioeconomic structures of life to be very concerned with that which
might lie beyond the limits of these structures.

And thus, although the majority of the issues related to the developmental task of identity formation (e.g., sustaining self-discipline,
succeeding in school, relations with the opposite sex, enhancing social skills) have no overt "limit" character to them, these transitional
years in the life cycle begin to engage individuals in the cognitive

search for the limits of human certainty in issues of knowledge, truth, and meaning.

ERIKSON'S FIFTH STAGE

In keeping with the method established in the previous chapter, we will turn to Erik Erikson's eight-stage model of the life cycle to give us a brief orientation to the major mental and emotional themes of adolescence and early adulthood.

Stage 5
Approximate Age: 12–22
Acquiring a Sense of Identity
(while overcoming a sense of identity confusion)
A Realization of Fidelity

Achieving a stable personal identity is a lifelong task. The critical period in this process, however, is undoubtedly the late teens and early twenties. During these years the rate of mental and physiological maturation quickens considerably. This rapid development brings new feelings, new sensations, new desires, and new needs. For the first time it is possible to engage in abstract thinking processes and consider wide ranges of possible responses to any given situation. This also means that it is now possible fully and realistically to imagine what others are thinking. And this, in turn, breeds considerable self-consciousness about how others are perceiving and reacting to us. It is also now possible to conceive of ideal families, societies, and religions which stand in sharp contrast to the imperfect families, societies, and religions we encounter on a day-to-day basis. Finally, persons now become capable of constructing theories and philosophies of their own. These are the years of idealism, when it is believed that it is as possible to create a perfect world as it is to imagine one.

Adolescence witnesses the transition from childhood to adulthood and thus demands that the individual synthesize or integrate the wide variety of roles society will increasingly expect him or her to perform. Deciding which of these roles to accept occasions the crisis of this developmental period. Establishing a sense of "who I am" requires forging some kind of unity out of one's past, identifying with some but not all of one's former roles as student, friend, athlete, dancer, or member of various social cliques. And, even more importantly, it means making at least tentative decisions about the future. Deciding who I am at this age is bound part and parcel with deciding who I will be. Identities are gradually forged as career options are assessed. Persons are forced to ask themselves such fundamental questions as, Am I really smart enough to achieve these goals? Do I have enough patience to wait that long? Is that really something that I would find rewarding or is it something that I would do just to please my parents or achieve social prestige?

Achieving a realistic identity is a difficult task and one that will continue well into a person's thirties and forties. For one thing, in the final analysis our identity is what emerges in our interaction with both social and business environments. That is, there must finally be a match between what we think of ourselves and how others view us. This requires constant adjustment of both our self-image and our behavioral strategies in light of the feedback supplied by others. Erikson has noted that early difficulties in achieving a match between inner and outer sources of our identity can lead to unfortunate resolutions of this critical period. For example, some individuals have such a difficult time in eliciting positive reinforcement from their parents and peers that they drop out and form what Erikson calls "negative identities." Whether originally given these identities by themselves or by others, they come to accept labels such as "acid head," "loose," "freak," or "delinquent."

Acquiring a realistic identity imparts the virtue of fidelity. Fidelity is the ability to sustain loyalty to an important commitment despite inevitable urges to "jump horses" at every opportunity. Fidelity is the cornerstone or foundation of identity and the mark of maturity. It is also the precondition of true love.

THE NEED FOR IDEOLOGY

As Erikson's model indicates, one of the most important tasks confronting individuals in this turbulent stage of life is that of acquiring a unified set of beliefs or a philosophy of life capable of giving a convincing set of guidelines, rules, and principles for action. Erikson calls this the acquisition of an ideology. For Erikson, the word ideology means "a system of commanding ideas" that enables an individual to take a firm hold upon life and make confident decisions in the face of seeming ambiguity. An ideology offers a set of concepts that gives a unified, comprehensive explanation of how life operates and how individuals should chart their course through life. Ideologies meet the developmental need for a clear understanding of the nature and meaning of life and thus tend to elicit intense loyalty.

What ideologies afford youth is a cognitive tool by which to get a handle on life and to solidify their identity. A crucial element of identity formation is finding a match between how you perceive yourself and the ways in which others view you. Being able to maintain a consistent conception of oneself as well as maintaining a consistent impression on others requires the possession of an ideological outlook that not only tells one who he or she is, but also what actions and commitments are expected. As Erikson has written, "By 'ideological,' I mean here a highly charged attitude rooted essentially in a general need for a world view coherent enough to attract one's total commitment and to render forever unnecessary the upsetting swings in mood and opinion which once accompanied identity confusion."[2] In order to elicit this kind of thoroughgoing commitment, ideologies must appear to the individual as worthy of his or her fidelity. They must have an intellectually compelling force to them; that is, they must be consistent with existing scientific theory and contemporary cultural attitudes in such a way as "to make facts amenable to ideas, and ideas to facts, in order to create a world image convincing enough to support the collective and the individual sense of identity."[3]

Much as the infant confronts the disruption of continuous attachment to the nurturing parent by creating a safe "transitional space" into which she or he might trustingly engage life, so must the adolescent utilize nonrational mental processes to create an ideological matrix that can make life appear trustworthy and true. Religious faith, of course, is a primary source from which (or possibly in contrast to which) individuals turn their world into a living whole which they might meet in a mutually enhancing manner. This is especially true for those to whom the need for cognitive certainty carries with it an ultimacy that drives them to the "limiting" questions concerning the origin and meaning of human existence. Religion draws upon the deepest yearnings humans have for aligning their lives with that which is central to existence and symbolizes what *feels* profoundly true even though it is not demonstrable. From a psychological perspective, religious faith can thus be viewed as an ongoing expression of those psychological processes that make it possible for humans to venture forth into life on the basis of basic trust. As Erikson remarks, "It translates into significant words, images, and codes the exceeding darkness which surrounds man's existence, and the light which pervades it beyond all desert or comprehension."[4]

Religious faith operates within the emerging identity as an adaptive and integrating force. Because religion roots the meaning and purpose of life in the transcendental reality of God, it makes it possible for individuals to locate themselves and their actions within a larger frame of reference. Religious doctrines enable individuals to make confident choices about who they are, what they stand for, and what they stand against. Religious faith also frees individuals from being at the total mercy of events in the outer world. Instead of being subjected to every new external influence, they are prepared to bring their own set of values and goals to bear upon the interpretation of everyday life. This makes possible the kind of mature and self-controlled behavior that the psychologist Gordon Allport calls "propriate striving"—conduct motivated by self-chosen values rather than by environmental or instinctual forces. And, too, religious faith reinforces a positive sense of self-worth by aligning our personal identity and moral outlook with an understanding of God's creative activity in the world.

Ironically, the very time when a developing individual most needs the ideological aspects of religion is simultaneously the time when he or she is also likely to begin having doubts about the truth of religion and its relevance to life in the modern world. Many "secular" philosophies drawn from science, political theory, or utopian philosophy might well strike adolescents or young adults as far more helpful viewpoints from which to set about pursuing personal growth or curing social ills. Young persons also typically need to make commitments that in some way express independence from their parents and thereby demonstrate their own ability to make decisions about their lives. For this reason the "rebelliousness" of youth often expresses it-self in terms of a rejection of the parents' religious faith. Some individuals might respond to the psychological demands of identity formation by converting to a denomination or sect quite different from that of their parents; others might affirm their family's religion in an almost fanatical way and in so doing demonstrate the importance of their newly made decisions. Most individuals, however, simply become less interested in religion during their youth and temporarily postpone making any final decision about the meaning or truth of religion. In the meantime, they tend to find fragments of their identity from a variety of sources that strike them as both realistic and meaningful.

Whatever the individual's particular manner of achieving a firm ideological outlook on life, the demands of identity formation tend to prompt youth to examine the intellectual aspects of religion; it also compels them to subject religion to what might be called ideological critique. To be worthy of their devotion it must be tested by the standards of logic and reason, and weighed on the scales of scientific knowledge. During such inquiry and critical examination secondhand faith quickly breaks down. The process of individualizing the ready-made faith handed to one at an earlier stage in life accelerates under the impetus of intellectual doubt.

DOUBT AND THE INDIVIDUALIZATION
OF FAITH

Far from being the enemy of religious faith, doubt is often its greatest ally. For until secondhand faith is dismantled under the pressure of ever widening ranges of experience it is impossible for a more reflective faith to emerge. As Allport has written, "We may then say the mature religious sentiment is ordinarily fashioned in the workshop of doubt."[5] Doubt subjects the verbal realisms and childish credulity of secondhand faith to questions raised by one's own personal and educational experiences. And by cutting away those elements that are no longer personally meaningful, doubt assists the difficult process of individualizing faith to the point where it becomes a living reality rather than a set of dead beliefs in which one strains to profess belief.

Doubt arises for many reasons and in many contexts. Each can be seen to be naturally occurring experiences of the human life cycle. We might begin to examine a few of them by dividing them into the somewhat artificial categories of personal doubts, scientific doubts, and rational doubts. The first of these, personal doubts, occur in moments when older religious beliefs no longer appear to be reliable guides to life. This is especially true of those moments when our personal interests are no longer being served by our religious beliefs. In the midst of a personal tragedy such as when a parent or other close relative dies, the heart cries out with anguish and the felt-sense of having been dealt a terrible injustice. In these moments it is almost impossible to maintain belief in, much less devotional love for, an almighty God. Disbelief in the existence of a God or doubt concerning the goodness of God shatters older religious beliefs. Other personal experiences likewise dismantle confidence in simplistic religious ideas. The experience of learning that there is no Santa Claus, Tooth Fairy, or Easter Bunny carries over to belief in a God. After all, letters asking Santa Claus to bring presents in reward for our good behavior differ little from prayer. And once one's sincerity and trust have been proven "childish" for such belief, hesitation and doubt crowd in to protect us from further experiences of being proved foolish or naive. We might note that whereas earlier epochs in history attempted to counteract the tendencies toward personal doubt, modern culture seems to foster suspiciousness and hesitancy. Our educational systems reward critical reasoning and systematic doubt. Modern academic disciplines such as sociology and psychology encourage us to adopt reductionistic interpretations of life by looking "behind" the surface of events and discovering the "real" cause or problem. That is, modern individuals tend to respond to other persons' accounts of a religious experience with skepticism, doubt, or suspicion of ulterior motives.

Scientific doubt refers to the inevitable tension that arises between scientific and religious perspectives on the nature of reality. The tremendous progress made by the natural sciences during the last one hundred years has in many respects undermined conventional religious thought. The empirical method of ascertaining truth shows no tolerance for unexamined assumptions or dogmatic adherence to unsupported hypotheses. This tension comes to a focus in the long-standing controversy between evolutionary science and the biblical account of creation as a special act of a Supreme Being. Individuals must finally commit themselves to the factual superiority of one of the two approaches. Living in an age dominated by the technological marvels generated by scientific research, it is increasingly difficult for educated persons not to admit to disbelief in the reliability of the "factual knowledge" set forth in the Bible. Once this is acknowledged, the foundations of most conventional religious beliefs go too. Bible miracles, the divine origin of the Ten Commandments, and the stipulated requirements for salvation must now be thought through all over again without easy reliance upon scriptural authority. So, too, must the very conception of a Supreme Being who is alleged to be residing "up there" or "out there" just beyond our planet's cloud cover. An ordained bishop of the Anglican church, John A. T. Robinson, voiced this growing element of disbelief among churchgoers in a book entitled *Honest To God.* Robinson wrote that the more he listened to scientifically inclined humanists debating with biblically oriented Christians, the more he came to side with the criticisms of religion raised by the humanists. Robinson confessed that the whole drift of his education tended to make orthodox religious beliefs appear embarrassingly irrational. Conventional doctrines concerning God, he concluded, are "crude supranaturalisms" and in a modern, scientific age are not deserving of our belief. And although Robinson remained a committed clergyman in the Christian faith, he was only able to do so by following his doubts to their logical conclusion and in the process repudiating all of those aspects of his religious heritage that could not be accommodated to the scientific temper of our age.[6]

Rational doubt concerning religion can have many sources. One obvious source is our not-so-infrequent observations of the shortcomings of organized religion. Awareness that religious faith (or at least what parades as religious faith) continues to give rise to war, bigotry, and intolerance inevitably occasions doubt in the "truth" of religious beliefs. So, too, does our observation of hypocrisy on the part of churchgoers. Although these kinds of charges against the truth of religion are *ad hominem* arguments (i.e., aimed against the persons professing the beliefs and not the beliefs themselves), and thus do not logically refute religious belief, they nonetheless give rise to considerable hesitancy and doubt. Awareness of the role that cultural conditioning plays in shaping a person's religious beliefs also leads to rational doubts concerning any religion's possession of "absolute, eternal" truth. For example, most educated persons are aware that the ancient Greeks and Romans, whose way of life depended upon such things as safety at sea and protection in battle, worshiped gods of sea and battle, and that Native Americans, whose way of life depended upon hunting and gathering, worshiped gods of wind, rain, and hunt. It tends to follow that religions reflect a culture's attempt to express its fears, hopes, and aspirations in ritualistic and symbolic ways. In short, it is not so much that God created humans as it is that humans create their gods. This becomes all the more problematic when one learns that even one's own religious tradition is subject to the fluctuations of history. A doctrine considered heresy in one epoch becomes a part of orthodoxy in another; a piece of writing originally written by one person is later declared by a council of church officials to have been written instead by a "saint" so that common believers will accept it on authority as holy truth. Religion, while claiming to represent universal truth, can rationally be regarded as subject to the same kinds of social and historical conditioning processes as any other human institution.

THE TRIUMPH OF FAITH OVER DOUBT

Those who experience doubt are ordinarily so concerned with that which they have come to question or even stand *against* that they often overlook what it is they have come to stand *for.* Disbelief in the truth of an idea reveals one's commitment to standards of truth that are in some way being violated. Thus, for example, rejecting a particular religious idea because it lacks sound empirical evidence is but another way of declaring that one be true to those ideas, and only those ideas, that are squarely rooted in the common stock of verifiable human knowledge. Conviction that reason and personal experience must be relied upon in the search for truth is itself a faith. As Tennyson once wrote, "There lives more faith in honest doubt, believe me, than in half your creeds."[7]

Bishop Robinson, whose disbelief in a literal interpretation of scriptural passages describing God as a humanlike being "up there" led him to reject much of his religious heritage, soon realized that he was all the while affirming a personal belief that religion has nothing to fear from knowledge gained through every faculty of human knowing. Doubt, he confided, takes great courage because it forces one to acknowledge the great gap between what we truly believe and what we merely pay lip service to one hour a week while in church. The demand of intellectual honesty struck Robinson as the foundation of religious integrity and he concluded that he could only be honest *to God* by first being honest about what he could in good intellectual conscience claim to believe *about God*.[8] Importantly, the new conceptions of Christian faith that Robinson's doubt-inspired train of thought led him to continue to this day to help thousands of modern Americans find a religious outlook that is both spiritually nourishing and compatible with scientific thought.

One of the most influential Christian theologians of the twentieth century, Paul Tillich, went so far as to state emphatically that a dynamic religious faith necessarily contains an element of intellectual doubt.[9] Tillich believed that all too often faith comes to mean believing ideas for which there is insufficient evidence. He contended that this distorts faith by making religious faith look less than rational. Tillich countered that faith is instead more than rational: It is the condition in which individuals are "grasped" by something that confronts them as unconditional, ultimate, and in some way intrinsic to the life process itself. Faith, for Tillich, is not so much a noun as it is a verb. It is present in any human activity, whether religious in a formal sense or not, in which a person is responding to life in a way that is guided by his or her sense of an ultimate meaning from which all other human activities derive their meaning and significance. In other words, a dynamic faith is one that attempts to accord the particulars of one's life with the Presence or Power from which life emanates. A dynamic faith such as that described by Tillich must necessarily acknowledge a certain element of doubt concerning any and all doctrinal formulations. Since human language pertains to the conditioned rather than the unconditioned, the finite rather than the infinite, doctrines necessarily contain symbolic rather than literal truth.

As Tillich suggests, doubt is only incompatible with faith insofar as the word faith is wrongly understood to mean agreeing to believe that which one knows is impossible. When faith is instead understood as the conviction that wholeness and fulfillment can often be found by uniting ourselves with that power which is central to existence, then faith can be seen to be a spontaneously occurring feature of the many limit experiences encountered throughout the human life cycle. Thus faith, no less than doubt, can be stimulated by ongoing experience. Even as doubt dismantles a faith acquired secondhand and forces us to confront our beliefs more openly and honestly, faith can reassert and validate itself over and against doubt. As we shall see more clearly in chapters 3 and 4, a good many commonly recurring experiences prompt individuals to look for, and find, the "secret" to life's dilemmas in that which lies beyond the limits of sensory experience. For now it will suffice to point out that faith can reassert itself over and against personal, scientific, and rationalistic doubts in one of three principal ways—the pragmatic, the mystical, and the intellectual or contemplative.

The pragmatic validation of faith over doubt refers to the fact that every idea or belief we hold about life serves what might be called a guiding function. That is, we acquire ideas and beliefs as part of our attempt to adapt successfully to the various environments we inhabit. We view those ideas that lead to successful relationships with life to be important and true; those that do not appreciably assist us are considered either false or unimportant. Insofar as religious beliefs or practices appear to impart zest or meaning to our lives they rightfully warrant our recognition as valuable "hypotheses" concerning the ultimate nature of reality. Even though the utility of a belief does not logically prove its truth, it does suggest that the belief in some way corresponds to the structure of reality. For example, many individuals operate their cars without paying any attention to the amount of oil in their engines. It is not until the car ceases to perform properly that they begin to pay attention to that which lies "beyond" the outwardly visible hood of their cars. Even though they never come to understand the technical functions that oil performs, its pragmatic usefulness alone will warrant "belief" that it is a necessary guide to the successful operation of a car. In this same way, the fact that common human experience repeatedly verifies the pragmatic truth of religious beliefs alone is sufficient grounds to prompt us to act faithfully upon them even without logical proof.

The mystical validation of faith refers to those limit experiences in which individuals somewhat ineluctably find themselves confronted with nonsensory dimensions of reality. Insofar as an individual has direct experience of a presence or power beyond the limits of rational or sensory knowledge, he or she possesses empirical evidence for considering this nonphysical reality as a clue to the nature and meaning of life. Undoubtedly the strong importance that religion places on prayer, meditation, ritual, and various altered states of consciousness is precisely owing to their ability to afford individuals a first-hand experience of a spiritual More beyond the limits of ordinary waking thought.

The intellectual or contemplative validation of faith refers to the rational insight that the extrinsic properties of reality are not self-explanatory. Reason runs up against its own limit when it asks why it is that there is a universe at all. Philosophers call this "the religious question" because although reason can ask the question of its own origin, it is inherently incapable of deriving the answer. When searching for the most comprehensive framework of thought, reason itself begins to assume the posture of faith. For example, the concept of the First Cause of the universe brings the mind to the limits of reason as a guide to the nature or meaning of life. The First Cause does not confront the rational mind as yet another object (for then it, too, would already be created or caused to be) but rather as the ontological and cosmological presupposition of thought. This realization that reason is an inherently inadequate tool for relating ourselves to the intrinsic meaning or purpose of life forces us to acknowledge the "validity" of concepts that do not confine themselves to the limits of logical reason. And, as we shall see, nearly every tough moral and intellectual problem that we confront in life finally demands some guiding notion concerning the nature and meaning of reality that cannot be derived from reason alone.

THE MATURING OF FAITH

The major point of this chapter is that *if* religion is to provide the foundations for a mature identity, it must impart a mature ideological direction for the continuing development of personality. The irony here is that of all the aspects of our personalities, our religious

attitudes are likely to be the least mature. Because religion is thought
to be the proper subject matter of our churches and not of public education, religious education is more or less confined to catechism
classes and Sunday schools, which ordinarily end by the time persons
reach their early teens. Thus, while every other dimension of their
personalities becomes progressively more complex and mature, the
religious aspects remain at a junior-high level of sophistication. As a
consequence, a person's true ideological stance toward the world is
informed largely by nonreligious concepts, regardless of any lip service given to the importance of religion in their lives. The most obvious way this is done is to compartmentalize religion into a set of
beliefs that supposedly pertain to the "soul" or the "afterlife," but not
to such things as what kind of vocation we ought to pursue or what
kind of economic policies we ought to advocate. Neatly compart-
mentalized into a set of doctrines appropriate to one hour per week,
religion can remain at an intellectually immature level and be kept
isolated from the rest of a person's developing life. It will not, however, become a significant factor in his or her identity.

The psychologist Gordon Allport devoted considerable attention
to the course of religious development in the mature and productive
personality. Allport used criteria drawn from his work in the area of
personality theory to specify the attributes of a religious faith capable of guiding individuals to the highest levels of personal development. A mature religious faith, he concluded, must be (1) well-
differentiated, (2) dynamic, (3) productive of a consistent morality,
(4) both comprehensive and integral, and (5) heuristic.[10]

By well-differentiated Allport means that a mature religious sentiment is one in which reason plays a strong role. Its various parts are
differentiated such that some can be held strongly while others are
identified as less important. This is in contrast to the all-or-nothing
character of an immature religious outlook based upon blind acceptance of every aspect of the faith equally. Immature faith tends to be
defensive, intolerant, and readily stiffens for a fight. A differentiated
faith, on the other hand, can abandon some concepts if new learnings
warrant, while strengthening or emphasizing others. A differentiated
faith, in other words, is better organized and far more realistic. And,
importantly, as individuals begin to differentiate among the many
aspects of their religious heritage, they become aware of picking and

choosing. Differentiation thus fosters the individualizing process whereby what was formerly a secondhand faith is transformed into an outlook based upon personal experience and choice. In the process of differentiating among religious beliefs and practices a person gradually leaves behind a faith built solely on the basis of imitation and identification. Just as mature individuals must give up rigid allegiances such as "my parents are perfect" or "my country is always right" and learn to assess their commitments more realistically, so, too, must they learn to examine their religious heritage. The oversimplifications of childhood need to be supplemented by a willingness to recognize that religion also has its negative aspects insofar as it often induces escapism, superstitiousness, apathy, backwardness, irrational outlooks on life, and so forth. In the process, the essence of religious commitment is distilled to principles that can be flexibly maintained as the sphere of personal experience continues to widen.

Perhaps the biggest difference between a mature and an immature religious faith is the presence of a dynamic element. As Karl Marx observed, religious beliefs have a tendency to stifle human initiative. Being taught that we are dependent on a higher power and that only the afterlife really matters, many religious individuals become apathetic and escapist. Rather than tackling life's challenges realistically and energetically, they instead resort to prayer and an attitude of resignation. Consider, for example, the case of a woman whose husband abruptly divorced her at the age of fifty-two. Having spent her entire adult life as a housewife, she was now at a considerable disadvantage in finding suitable employment. She also found herself with few social companions as she no longer fit well into the activities of other married couples. After several months she made an appointment with her minister to express her dismay that God had sent her such misery and suffering. She proclaimed that she still had as much faith in God as ever, but could not understand why he was not answering her prayers. When the minister inquired about whether she had typed up a resume, taken skill-development courses at the local community college, called acquaintances to get job leads, or attended any of the social functions at her apartment complex, she responded no but that she read her Bible and prayed every day for God to send her a job and more friends. Certainly, she reasoned, if God could part the Red Sea, he could send these small requests to someone as faithful as she. As the minister quickly realized, this woman's religious beliefs were stifling the personality strengths Erikson calls will, purpose, and competence. Only by first helping her to realize that the divine life works through, not around, the total organization of personality could he begin to help her express her faith more dynamically.

In contrast to the indifference and escapist tendencies often found in immature faith, the strongest and most fully developed manifestations of religion give rise to an impassioned approach to life. Firsthand religious faith can be recognized by its mood of welcome and tendency to view active service to others as a privilege rather than a burdensome duty. As William James noted, "It makes a tremendous emotional and practical difference to one whether one accept the universe in the drab discolored way of stoic resignation to necessity, or with the passionate happiness of Christian saints. The difference is as great as that between passivity and activity, as that between the defensive and the aggressive mood."[11]

A third characteristic of religious maturity is the consistency of its moral directives. The relationship between morality and religion is a complex one. While the former has to do with our relationships with fellow human beings, the latter has to do with our relatedness to that which lies beyond the limits of ordinary sensory experience. Of course, those persons who equate religious faith with obedience to Scripture see a direct connection between the two. This connection, however, is not nearly so direct as it might appear. A view that restricts "religious morality" to what is written in Scripture is guilty of compartmentalizing faith by restricting it to an isolated set of behaviors. What is more, this view breaks down quickly when one takes the perspective of the comparative study of world religions. From this perspective, the fact that every culture possesses its own set of sacred writings implies that they are little more than the mythological writings of ancient cultures; the values they uphold reflect the customs of premodern, prescientific people and cannot be applied directly to modern life. The point here is that it is not clear that there really is such a thing as a set of "religious ethics." Ethical principles reflect rational approaches to human relationships and by no means depend upon religious beliefs. But insofar as ethical concepts often call upon us to sacrifice our own personal good for the good of others, either now or in the remote future, they call for us to be committed to a point of view that requires us to go beyond the perspective of our own limited personality. As Allport observes, "Ethical standards are difficult to sustain without idealism; and idealism is difficult to sustain without a myth of Being."[12] By providing the ideological foundations of an identity that can view itself *sub specie aeternitatas,* religious faith potentially makes possible the most strenuous of all ethical commitments.

As we have already noted, a prime characteristic of a psychologically immature faith is that of compartmentalization. Religion of this type is associated with a distinct set of beliefs and practices that are clearly set off from the rest of one's life. In such a view religion is thought to pertain to the afterlife, a Supreme Being, church attendance, and so forth; yet the rest of one's life is interpreted in the categories of secular culture as though these aspects of life are in some way not expressions of the human spirit (and consequently of the divine life itself). In contrast, a mature faith infects every area of life with a sense of participating in, and contributing to, the unfolding of the cosmos. A comprehensive religious faith seeks to understand how each and every facet of human existence corresponds to that which is central to existence. It therefore embraces knowledge from every sphere of life and affirms the ultimate unity of truth. Not only does this demand for comprehensiveness lead to a faith which is corational and coscientific, it also instills the fundamental attitudes of humility and tolerance. The very attempt to incorporate every last aspect of the world's experience into a unified perspective forces the humbling recognition that no one person's knowledge is fully adequate. Because of our educational, cultural, and historical limitations we can never hope to reduce religious faith to a single intellectual formulation. Other persons, approaching the issue of humanity's relationship to the "More" of finite existence from other cultural and educational perspectives, must therefore be appreciated for what they can potentially contribute to our ongoing search.

This demand for comprehensiveness simultaneously implies that a mature faith must be heuristic. That is, it views religion not as a closed system of doctrines but as a journey, a quest. The mature religious faith always seeks more light. Every new idea is embraced as a working hypothesis that might potentially be useful in disclosing our relationship to the divine. Inspired to comprehend how the physical participates in the metaphysical, a heuristic faith has an open, eager, fresh quality.

Allport's criteria of religious maturity are helpful in that they draw attention to the fact that religion needs to be assessed according to its ability to foster a psychologically strong identity. It might be mentioned, however, that Allport's criteria pertain primarily to the ideological (i.e., the intellectual) aspects of religion. They omit considerations of the experiential bases of a mature faith. The noted American psychologist William James held theories about religious maturity very similar to Allport's, but additionally insisted that a firsthand faith must also include a mystical dimension. According to James, religion never becomes an independent force within the total structure of personality until individuals develop a lived sense of an unseen order of things. Insofar as faith means the conviction that the visible world is a part of a wider spiritual universe, it is dependent upon a peculiar range of experiences that go beyond the "limit" of ordinary sense perception. A mature faith, then, must also include active concern for those kinds of activities such as prayer, ritual, and meditation that can help individuals cultivate an awareness of the continuity between their lives and a higher spiritual universe. It is then, and only then, that faith can become a dynamic hypothesis for living based on the premise that communion with the More of psychic life produces beneficial effects within the human realm.

FOWLER'S RESEARCH ON
FAITH DEVELOPMENT

James Fowler has produced a wealth of empirical research that substantiates the concept that faith, as with every other aspect of personality, is subject to a lawful developmental process. Fowler's model of faith development is a structural model closely resembling that of the noted cognitive psychologist Jean Piaget. Structural models focus much less on the content of a person's ideas than the psychological structures that underlie them. They classify types or stages of faith not according to *what* is believed, but according to *how* beliefs are organized into structures and how these structures correspond to the person's other ideas and knowledge about life. For this reason Fowler tends to view faith as a verb rather than as a noun. Faith is a "way of knowing." It is a way of construing or interpreting one's experience in terms of one's relation to the ultimate conditions of existence.

> In this sense faith is a knowing, or construing which fixes on the related-ness of a person or a community to power(s), boundaries (such as death and finitude), and source(s) of being, value and meaning which impinge on life in a manner not subject to personal control. In theological language, faith is the knowing or construing by which persons apprehend themselves as related to the Transcendent.[13]

By focusing on the structures according to which individuals interpret their relationship to life's ultimate boundaries, Fowler has discovered that faith development proceeds through seven distinct stages. Progress through these stages is to some extent age-determined. Fowler has detected what would appear to be minimum ages associated with movement between each successive stage. These are, however, minimum ages and it must be emphasized that each individual develops at his or her own rate as life circumstances allow. And, as we shall see, few individuals are ever afforded the kinds of experiences that would enable them to move to the later stages of faith development. The kind of ideological structure faith imparts to our identity is thus determined by the psychological characteristics of the final stage of faith development to which we obtain. Clearly Fowler's concept of faith development captures only the cognitive organization of beliefs and does not embrace other aspects of the religious life such as prayer, mystical insight, the development of compassion, and so forth. Nor does his model fully make allowances for many variables which differentiate individuals by gender, economic class, and exposure to Western educational and cultural influences. Nonetheless, his stages of faith development offer us a helpful model for understanding the difficult process whereby religious beliefs acquired early in human life gradually become differentiated into "a way of knowing" capable of leading individuals to profound levels of maturity and insight.

A brief overview of the stages Fowler detected in the course of faith development will help illustrate the relationship between faith, ideology, and identity formation.[14] These stages reveal a distinct developmental process; Fowler's studies indicate that a person cannot move to a higher stage until the preceding one has been successfully appropriated into his or her personality. Each stage builds on the preceding stages and, in turn, lays the foundation for subsequent stages. The order of development through these stages is invariant. Everyone follows the same sequence of development, although some individuals pass through a given stage more rapidly than others. Since each of the seven stages is the last stage reached by many individuals, they can be thought of as "types" of religiously-grounded identities.

Stage One: Primal Faith. Closely corresponding to Erikson's stage of trust versus mistrust, this stage refers to an infant's relationships with parents and others insofar as they give rise to prelinguistic dispositions of trust or anxiety (infancy).

Stage Two: Intuitive-Projective Faith. Beginning about the age of four, children begin to acquire religious ideas through imitation and identification. This is an imitative, fantasy-filled phase in which the child can be powerfully and permanently influenced by the examples, moods, and actions of the visible religious practices of adults. Stories, gestures, and symbols, not yet controlled by logical thinking, combine to create long-lasting images about the powers that govern life (early childhood).

Stage Three: Mythic-Literal Faith. The developing ability to think logically helps the individual to order his or her world with help of the stories, beliefs, and observance that symbolize belonging to his or her community. As part of adapting to this community the individual adopts its attitudes and moral rules. Religious ideas are one-dimensional and literal. Parental authority still counts for more than the opinions of peers (childhood and beyond).

Stage Four: Synthetic-Conventional Faith. The person's experience of the world is now extended beyond the family and primary social groups. The social environment now includes family, school and/or work, peers, and possibly a religious congregation. Faith must help provide a coherent and meaningful synthesis of this diverse range of involvements. The individual seeks some kind of mental and emotional solidarity with others by submitting to the authority in each of his or her social spheres. The individual has not yet taken on the burden of world-synthesis for himself or herself (adolescence and beyond).

Stage Five: Individuating-Reflexive Faith. The transition from stage four to stage five begins if and when the individual begins to take seriously the burden of responsibility of his or her own morals, beliefs, lifestyle, or intellectual standards of truth. Critical reflection upon the "proof" behind conventional religious faith forces the individual to face certain intellectual tensions which the submission to authority characteristic of stage four allowed him or her to evade: the relative versus the absolute, the individual versus the community, self-fulfillment versus service to others, the demands of reason versus the need for emotional security. This stage requires a qualitatively new and different kind of self-awareness and responsibility for one's choices and rejections. It is often vulnerable to popular cultural trends, charismatic individuals, and powerful ideological perspectives that resolve the kinds of tensions noted above by clearly advocating one side of these questions and repudiating the other (young adulthood and beyond).

Stage Six: Paradoxical-Consolidative Faith. In stage five the person is self-conscious about making commitments and knows something of what is being denied or excluded as choices are made. But the kinds of choices made in stage five tend to be made by focusing upon only one side of each argument at the expense of acknowledging the important truths expressed in the rejected point of view. Stage six represents an advance in that it recognizes the integrity and truth in positions other than its own. Stage six recognizes that life itself contains polarities. It is alert to paradox and the need for multiple interpretations of reality. Symbols, myths, scientific method, logical analysis, and scriptural stories—some of which were necessarily repudiated in stage five—are newly appropriated as complementary vehicles for grasping truth. Stage six is also ready for community beyond that of tribal, class, or ideological boundaries. To be genuine this need must acknowledge the self-sacrificing cost of such community and be prepared to translate values and beliefs into risk and action (midlife and beyond).

Stage Seven: Universalizing Faith. Stage seven is rare. These are the few individuals who come to actualize what Jews and Christians call the kingdom of God and what the Buddha called selfless identification with all that lives. Although these individuals are transforming actors *in* the world, in some fundamental way they are not *of* the world. In stage six (consolidating faith) commitment to a universal community remained paradoxical. Affirming others still entailed denying oneself. Loyalties were still distorted by investment in tribe, class, nation, ideological preferences, and so forth. In stage seven individuals begin to experience, and know themselves to be participating in, the Ultimate. Such individuals experience the "power of being" as a live, felt reality and thus know themselves to be members of a cosmic community. These rare individuals are ready for fellowship with persons at any of the other stages and from any other faith tradition. They are devoted to overcoming oppression, brutality, and divisions of all kinds. They seem instinctively to know how to relate to others affirmingly, never condescendingly, and to point us to the sacred dimension ever present in our own midst.

Religion will, of course, not be a component of every person's developing identity. At least not in the first half of the life cycle. But insofar as religious faith does impart the ideological foundations of our personality structures, it comes under a series of developmental pressures, as is indicated in Fowler's studies. A glance back over the seven stages of faith development reveals a startling fact: Religion of a living or firsthand kind is developmentally related to the tasks and challenges of the second half of the life cycle.

THREE

VALUES AND MIDLIFE TRANSITIONS

The developmental challenges faced in the second half of the life cycle are far less concerned with adapting successfully to the material and social environments. Instead, adults find themselves vitally involved in such activities as caring for a new generation, making the world "right," discovering the meaning and purpose of their existence, or confronting their approaching death. Successfully meeting challenges such as these requires sensitivity to structures of existence that are not "out there" in any simple or straightforward sense. For this reason, adult fulfillment depends increasingly less upon extrinsic measures of worth and increasingly more upon an awareness of participating in activities intrinsic to life itself. And, as we shall see, the search for wholeness in the second half of life inevitably draws our attention to what we have called the limit dimension of human existence and thus demands that we learn to engage life in what are essentially religious ways.

ERIKSON'S SIXTH AND SEVENTH STAGES

The attainment of a sense of individual identity more or less coincides with a dramatic shift in one's location in the ongoing cycle or sequence of generations. While it is perhaps impossible to pinpoint the exact moment we make the transition from adolescence to adulthood, the transition is nonetheless real and in many ways abrupt. Responsibilities rapidly begin to outweigh freedoms. Support and nurturance are less likely to be forthcoming from one's parents or childhood peers and must instead be found in newly formed adult relationships. New patterns of relating to life must be discovered that take into account the loss of youthful dependency. Sustained fulfillment and happiness require the acquisition of the more self-extending virtues of love and care.

Stage 6
Age: Young Adulthood
Acquiring a Sense of Intimacy
(while avoiding a sense of isolation)
A Realization of Love

The sixth stage of the life cycle is young adulthood; roughly the period of courtship, marriage, and early parenting years. Erikson describes this as the period in which an individual will either learn to love and be intimate with another person or else risk going forward through life in relative isolation. When Erikson speaks of intimacy he means much more than physical lovemaking. Erikson is referring to the ability to share with, and care about, another person without fear of losing oneself in the process. Intimacy, then, is love without defensiveness and without continual preoccupation with oneself. If the capacity for intimacy is not established with a close friend or marriage partner, the individual becomes increasingly isolated from the social mainstream and soon finds her- or himself with no one to share with or care for.

The major developmental theme of this period involves psychological readiness for the commitments entailed in marriage. Readiness for intimacy includes the ability, and even more so the desire, to share mutual trust, to regulate periods of work, recreation, and procreation for each partner's fullest satisfaction.

The virtue established during this stage is that of love. Love is the mutuality in devotion that continually overcomes the friction and antagonisms that appear when two persons are divided in their commitments. Love guarantees that individual identity is retained in joint intimacy, and binds two persons together into a "way of life" over and beyond their separate identities.

Stage 7
Approximate Age: Middle Age
Acquiring a Sense of Generativity
(and avoiding a sense of self-absorption)
A Realization of Care

The previous two stages, those of achieving a personal identity and establishing intimacy with a spouse or friend, were stages of maximum freedom and minimum responsibility (e.g., college life, when students are responsible to and for no one but themselves). But now the individual begins to participate in the wider business and social communities. He or she begins a career, becomes a neighbor, and establishes a home. Adult liberty brings with it adult responsibility.

The tasks and challenges of this long stage require us to expand our conception of the "cycle" of life. Up to now we have viewed the life cycle as the span of years from birth to death. There is, however, another meaning of the cycle of life. This is the cycle not of our individual lives, but of entire generations. Every generation cogwheels with those preceding and following it. While in youth the quality of our individual lives is dependent upon what we receive from an older generation; in maturity our happiness and fulfillment are in large part determined by how we "recycle" our lives in our offspring and their new generation. The concept of the life cycle is thus in many ways similar to the biological concept of ecology. It, too, invokes the idea of an ecosystem in which all the separate living organisms are ultimately interconnected. The human ecosystem, like biological ecosystems, links each of its members together into an organic whole. The actions of each member of the system have long-term consequences in terms of the readiness of the environment to nurture healthy development. The fact that our separate lives are in the final analysis thoroughly intertwined with the lives of others gives added poignancy to Erikson's notion of the golden rule (i.e., his insight that the social nature of all personal development links enlightened self-interest with ethical responsibility).

The seventh stage of the life cycle is characterized by responsibility for the care of the next generation. What Erikson calls "generativity" is the concern with others beyond one's immediate family, with future generations and the nature of the world in which they will live. Generativity is thus separate from biological parenting per se. It concerns actively caring for the welfare of others, especially for the young, by making the world a better place in which to live. Those who fail to establish a sense of generativity fall into a state of self-absorption in which their personal needs and comforts are of predominant concern.

This is the ethical stage of life. Each adult accepts or rejects the moral responsibility of assuring a new generation a world that can elicit their basic trust. It is thus understandable that many individuals, often for the first time, begin in this stage to ask themselves the "big questions": Is life inherently meaningful, and if so, why? What should be imparted into a young child's values, and why? What ultimately counts in life, and why? Has anything I have ever done been truly important, and if so, why? These questions, by taking us beyond empirical facts about life's details and to the "limits" of rational inquiry, begin to point individuals beyond ethical questions to religious ones. Institutional religion often becomes more important to individuals at this stage. It offers symbols that confidently affirm the grounds for trust in life and offers a fund of moral teachings to offer the next generation. Church communities provide a context that regulates the successful commitment to this critical stage where life cycles, and generations of life cycles, intersect.

Generativity gives rise to the virtue of care. Care is the widening concern for what has been generated by love, necessity, or accident. Care overcomes the ambivalence most persons have about their obligation to their offspring and the future. Erikson deplores the general lack of this virtue in modern society. The fundamental problem of modern individuals, Erikson believes, is their inability to care for what they create, what they generate. We see this in the way modern parents treat their children, the way we build our buildings, conduct science, ravish the environment, and experiment with technology. Erikson counsels that what makes us truly generative beings is not the quantity of what we create, but rather the quality of our sustained care for that which we have created.

PATTERNS OF ADULT DEVELOPMENT

In recent years there has been an outpouring of literature concerning midlife developmental stages.[1] While largely reconfirming Erikson's general scheme, these studies have added a great deal of additional insight into the changing nature of personal fulfillment across the life span. Daniel Levinson's often-cited *Seasons of a Man's Life* is perhaps the most helpful of these accounts of midlife transitions.[2] Although Levinson's study focused on middle-class American males and is thus in need of critical reassessment through the balancing vision of theorists such as Carol Gilligan, it nonetheless helps us to map the major phases of adult development.[3] Levinson suggests that middle age consists of two distinct eras: early adulthood, which covers the approximate age span of twenty-two to forty, and middle adulthood which begins at about forty and continues to the age of sixty, when one leaves middle age and enters late adulthood (which we will examine in the next chapter). Early adulthood begins as the individual in his or her early twenties begins to enter the world of adult vocational and familial responsibilities. This is a time when initial decisions must be made about one's occupation, love relationships, marriage possibilities, and preferred life style. Levinson's studies revealed that decisions such as these usually coincide with the formulation of a "dream." This dream symbolizes a person's major aspirations and, therefore, values concerning the ideal state of personal fulfillment. Usually this dream has to do with vocational and economic success and is defined largely in terms of promotions, income, status, and social influence. A major part of the rest of adult development will have to do with making adjustments and modifications in this dream to accommodate better the concrete experiences encountered along life's way.

The transition between early and middle adulthood comes in subtle ways. For the most part, the transition consists of growing awareness of a gradual diminishment in one's bodily vigor combined with periods of doubt and partial dissatisfaction with the unfolding of one's chosen dream. By our early forties, our muscle tissue is no longer as supple and resilient as in our youth. It is not uncommon for women to find their hips and thighs going soft despite their best efforts and for men to watch their hair thin and a paunch begin to grow around their midsection, which is seemingly impervious to dietary regimens or exercise. Eyesight, too, begins to weaken and many begin to need reading glasses. Birthdays have long since ceased being milestones in the process of growing up, and are now markers of how fast we are growing old. This time in life witnesses a discernible shift in our location within the sequence of generations. Younger colleagues come to ask advice, one's children are now old enough to face adult questions and challenges themselves. Perhaps one of the most significant developmental challenges of this period is the inevitable reversal of roles between parent and child. Somewhere in middle age, adults typically find themselves "parenting" their parents; helping make financial decisions, moving them to smaller apartments or nursing homes, attending them during serious illness and death. There is no longer an older generation in the work place or neighborhood to turn to for assurance and comfort; these must now be found within. In other words, basic trust in life cannot be acquired from older authority figures any longer and must instead by found through one's personal reflections on life.

While in your twenties and early thirties life seems all out in front of you; infinite possibilities, unending chances to start all over and try something new. By the late thirties unlimited possibilities have largely given way to one or two fairly narrow paths. The necessities of child care, mortgage payments, and responsibilities toward one's spouse's preferred life style make it all but impossible to make sudden changes. The feeling of being "trapped" is not uncommon. And, too, for the first time a person is in a position to predict his or her economic and vocational future with reasonable accuracy. Careers are sufficiently established that one's position on the ladder leading to "the top" is evident. Most of us must finally realize that our dream will never quite come true. As the dream undergoes a radical assault it simultaneously becomes modified and adjusted to more realistic paths toward self-fulfillment. With this change in our valued ideal life come many perplexing questions: Who am I? What have I done with my life? What do I get from my job, my spouse, my family? What do I give to my job, my spouse, my family? In the years that I have left, what do I most want to accomplish and do I want to remain committed to the persons and tasks I am currently tied to?

None of this, however, detracts from the possibility and even likeli-

hood that these years will constitute the prime of life. Securing a vocational identity can bring a sense of accomplishment and pride. A
family brings excitement and endless opportunities to feel loved and
needed. Experience and accumulated knowledge more than make up
for the waning of youthful exuberance. Indeed, this is the period in
which most professional advancements take place. And, as Levinson
has shown, this is also the period during which individuals are most
capable of growing beyond the socially conditioned aspects of their
personalities and displaying increasing degrees of individuality and
uniqueness. Noting that his studies confirm Jung's theory of the
midlife "individuation process," Levinson argues that it is not until
our forties that we are truly capable of disentangling ourselves from
the socialization process, so that our growth can instead become
truly inner-directed.

But what needs to be underscored is the inevitable sense of limitation that accompanies finally finding one's place in life. The awareness that one's basic life script has by now been largely written will
inevitably be accompanied by a certain amount of regret concerning
roads that will never be traveled. No longer are we contemplating the
lives we might live when we grow up, but rather are struggling to
make the most out of the one path we must now irreversibly follow to
its end.

MIDLIFE CRISES AS
LIMIT EXPERIENCES

A great many books have been written in recent years about how
one might go about confronting midlife crises (e.g., the lure of extra-
marital affairs, divorce, menopause, the transition to the empty nest,
career disappointment) in growth-enhancing ways.[4] What is often
missing in these psychological accounts of midlife crises is an explicit recognition of their broadly spiritual character. They are not
simply continuations of the same kind of psychological adjustments
faced in one's teens and twenties. Instead, they entail a yearning to
achieve meaning and to accord one's life with something that transcends the ambiguities of day-to-day life. Midlife developmental
challenges cannot be solved through the kind of instrumental reason-

ing processes that enable us to set career objectives and master the successive tasks to bring us to that goal. Rather than being concerned with finding means to a socially defined end, they entail making personal decisions about which "ends" are worth pursuing. In midlife we find ourselves searching not for extrinsic measures of success, but for guides to life's intrinsic values and meanings.

It was precisely this shift from material to spiritual frames of reference that the famed psychologist Carl Jung had in mind when he observed that his patients over thirty-five "all have been people whose problem in the last resort was that of finding a religious outlook on life."[5] What Jung referred to is the fact that nearly every midlife crisis can be reduced to the individual's need for what might be called a "myth of Being" capable of imparting guidelines for confident choice and action. By middle adulthood it becomes apparent that we cannot accomplish an infinite number of things in a single lifetime. There will always be unfinished tasks, new roads to travel, new possessions to acquire. Thus, what is needed is some kind of perspective from which to sort out and arrange life's many opportunities and experiences into some kind of pattern that will reveal which ones are ultimately worth pursuing. The underlying developmental challenge of middle age, then, is that of finding an outlook or vision that can assess various courses of conduct not according to their external measures of worth, but rather according to their ability to contribute to the actualization of meanings and values that can be affirmed to have an intrinsic significance over and beyond the span of a single human life.

The vast majority of midlife crises, then, can potentially lead individuals to a profound consideration of the limit dimension of the meaning and purpose of life. Consider, for example, individuals who in their thirties or forties begin to question whether the career they chose earlier in life is really right for them. A successful attorney or accountant might begin wondering whether she should instead have pursued an earlier inclination to be a high school teacher. Or, a school teacher might find himself wondering whether he and his family wouldn't have been better off had he instead become an attorney earning three or four times his current salary. In either case the "developmental challenge" cannot be mastered simply by acquiring yet another professional skill; nor can it be resolved through means-end reasoning processes. Rather, it induces the individual to begin asking a series of questions that leads to ontological, metaphysical, and spiritual considerations of the meaning of life. He or she begins by asking, What do I really want to do with my life? This question invariably leads to a consideration of what *should* a person want to do with his or her life. This in turn leads to an attempt to view human life from "above" as it were and ask, Why are we here anyway and what are we meant to do with our lives? What began as an attempt to evaluate the relative trade-off between two careers leads inevitably to the need for an outlook on life capable of orienting us to the very meaning and purpose of our universe. Only by first gaining some sense of the intrinsic value of human life can we begin to sort out and make confident decisions about which of life's many possible paths we ought to pursue. Midlife dilemmas about one's chosen career are thus not so much about occupation as they are about what theologians mean by "vocation"; that is, they have to do with determining what purposes and activities are truly worth advancing, and being able to claim confidently that one's own efforts have in some way contributed toward this end.

The change in one's fundamental posture toward life brought about by adult dilemmas is, as Jung describes, the beginning of a reversal in the values we hold concerning the nature of human fulfillment.

> The noon of life is the moment of greatest deployment, when a man is devoted entirely to his work, with all his ability and all his will. But it is also the moment when the twilight is born: the second half of life is beginning. . . . At midday the descent begins, determining a reversal of all the values and all the ideals of the morning.[6]

Midlife begins what Jung calls the "individuation process" whereby the socially defined ego gradually gives way to a wider, though unconscious, range of potentials that constitute the true core of selfhood. Individuation can begin only to the extent that the individual no longer looks to the outer world as the primary source of his or her identity and values. According to Jung, wholeness is not possible for adults who approach life only in terms of rational efforts to adapt to the outer environment. Our highest possibilities are mediated to us through the unconscious. Importantly, Jung distinguished between what he termed the "personal unconscious" (i.e., the repository of our instinctual desires and forgotten memories) and the "collective unconscious." In an effort to distinguish his theory of psychological causation from "material," "environmental," or even "final" arguments, Jung contended that the collective unconscious transcends the biological, social, and psychological dimensions of existence and contains the basic patterns (archetypes) and energies by which the individuation process proceeds.

The collective unconscious is, furthermore, transpersonal in nature in that it constitutes a psychic network or medium through which each and every human being is ultimately connected not only with one another but also with the creative power of the universe (God). Thus, according to Jung the essential challenge of midlife is to acquire values and living habits that enable the collective unconscious to begin manifesting itself through the now developed personality. The route to personal wholeness and well-being thus becomes increasingly an inner rather than outer one. It requires contemplation, introspection, and a "letting go" of the intuitions and inspirations of the God within. Fulfillment in the latter half of the life cycle proceeds upon our realization that our highest Self is not achieved by seeking to impose our desires on socioeconomic spheres. Rather, we must learn to let go of our socially defined persona and thereby allow the creative possibilities of our unconscious to manifest themselves in our lives unobstructed by previous ego identifications. Viewed in this way, the final stages of human fulfillment come not by struggling against the outer world but by letting go to a Higher Self. This, Jung contended, is an essentially religious as opposed to secular approach to life.

There is, then, a sense in which the underlying theme of most midlife crises is implicitly religious.[7] The tough intellectual questions and moral dilemmas of this stage of life increasingly demand that the individual confront the limit dimension of human experience as a prerequisite to personal integration. For this reason Erikson speaks of the important way "in which every human being's Integrity may be said to be religious."[8] The effort to attain a perspective from which life can be seen as unified and whole is in the final analysis "an inner search for, and wish to communicate with, that mysterious, that Ultimate Other: for there can be no 'I' without an 'Other,' no 'We' without a shared 'Other.'"[9]

SUSTAINING CARE: FROM MORALITY
TO METAPHYSICS

Adult health and fulfillment, as Erikson points out, do not depend upon further development of the sense of individual identity so much as they do upon establishing relationships of care with others. Acquiring a sense of generativity entails actively caring for the welfare of others, especially for the young, by making the world a better place for them to live and work. Each and every adult is confronted with the moral responsibility of assuring the new generation the sense of basic trust and adaptive strengths necessary for their continued well-being. Successfully meeting this moral challenge requires avoiding what William James called the "easy-going mood" and acquiring instead the "strenuous mood."[10] Whereas the easy-going mood is ruled by pursuit of immediate personal pleasure, the strenuous mood is one in which we are quite indifferent to our personal sacrifices provided that the greater good be attained. The strenuous mood thus elicits our willingness both to sacrifice our personal interests for the sake of others and to forgo immediate satisfactions in favor of future generations.

The capacity for the strenuous moral life, however, is a developmental achievement rather than an inherited disposition. It builds upon the individual's efforts to transcend the limits of his or her own finite personality and instead to assume a universal perspective of the requirements of moral conduct. For this reason James observed the strong relationship between the development of strenuous moral commitments and the development of religious belief. Our moral consciousness postulates and reaches out for a God through whom we can come to feel intimately identified with our fellow living creatures and in terms of whose demands we are prompted to take seriously the requirements of the remote future. A purely humanistic world view, James notes, can never elicit the intensity of identification with others and with future generations necessary to sustain a strenuous moral life. He writes,

> This too is why, in a merely human world without a God, the appeal to our moral energy falls short of its maximal stimulating power. . . . [most of us] would openly laugh at the very idea of the strenuous mood being awakened in us by those claims of remote posterity which constitute the

last appeal of the religion of humanity. We do not love these men of the future strongly enough. . . . When, however, we believe that a God is there, and that he is one of the claimants, the infinite perspective opens out. The scale of the symphony is incalculably prolonged. The more imperative ideals now begin to speak with an altogether new objectivity and significance, and to utter the penetrating, shattering, tragically challenging note of appeal.[11]

James maintained that even if there were no reason for believing in God other than the demands imposed by ethical necessity, the emergence of religious faith in the fully rational adult is yet justified by its own evolutionary-adaptive functions: "Every sort of energy and endurance, of courage and capacity for handling life's evils, is set free in those who have religious faith [and thus for] this reason the strenuous type of character will on the battle-field of human history always outwear the easy-going type, and religion will drive irreligion to the wall."[12]

The twentieth-century philosopher Alfred North Whitehead similarly observed that religion emerges out of the "longing of the spirit that the facts of existence should find their justification in the nature of existence."[13] That is, our moral consciousness postulates God as the precondition of meaningful ethical conduct. Unless there is a power or lawfulness underlying the universe, then all of our moral efforts are but vanity. If we do not postulate God, then we must admit that the universe may well be indifferent, or perhaps even hostile, to the demands of adult care. As the personality theorist Gordon Allport points out, "Ethical standards are difficult to sustain without idealism; and idealism is difficult to sustain without a myth of Being."[14] And while the emergence and "usefulness" of religious belief amidst the generative functions of middle age in no way prove the truthfulness of these beliefs, they nevertheless clarify how readily the limit dimension of common human experience points us toward metaphysical considerations of human existence.

Lawrence Kohlberg's noted studies of the stages of moral development further substantiate the limit dimension or religious character of midlife moral challenges. Kohlberg's studies indicate that the experiences of sustained care for the welfare of others and of the irreversibility of so many of our moral choices are often accompanied by a haunting doubt: Why be moral? Kohlberg has observed that even in

those individuals who have attained a clear awareness of universal
ethical principles there is yet a loud skeptical doubt concerning why,
in a universe that is largely unjust, should we commit ourselves to a
universal rather than egoistic ethical perspective.[15] Importantly,
Kohlberg further notes that

> the answer to the question "Why be moral?" at this level entails the
> question "Why live?" (and the parallel question, "How face death?") so
> that ultimate moral maturity requires a mature solution to the question
> of the meaning of life. This, in turn, is hardly a moral question per se; it
> is an ontological or a religious one. Not only is the question not a moral
> one but it is not a question resolvable on purely logical or rational
> grounds as moral questions are.[16]

The "logic" of ultimate moral maturity, says Kohlberg, is that
which pertains to the structure of religious rather than rational experience; it emerges from the grasping of a metaphysical or cosmic
perspective rather than logically analyzing life from a physical or
humanistic perspective. Comparing the state of mind that finally
recognizes life's intrinsic moral fabric to what Spinoza called "the
union of the mind with the whole of nature," Kohlberg found that
attaining the pinnacle of moral development involves mystical or
contemplative experiences in which the ego is transcended en route
to the acquisition of a cosmic perspective. He writes, "The logic of
such experience is sometimes expressed in theistic terms, but it
need not be. Its essential is the sense of being a part of the whole of
life and the adoption of a cosmic, as opposed to a [purely humanis-
tic] perspective."[17]

THE SEARCH FOR MEANING

The paramount concerns of middle age are no longer those of identity, but rather of sustaining care and discovering the basis of integrity. The major question underlying our many worries and doubts is
not that of Who am I? but What does it all mean? We find ourselves
wondering what kind of life we really ought to be making for ourselves. Who do we want to be with for the rest of our lives and how do
we want to be with them? To what work do we wish to devote ourselves in the years we have remaining? The decisions we make about

these kinds of questions are irreversible. We have but one life cycle to live and we are now determining its overall purpose and design. The need to establish an identity has given way to the need to discover whether this identity has any ultimate value or meaning. The importance of the "search for meaning" in adult life has been eloquently described in the writings of psychologist Viktor Frankl. Frankl argues that humans live in three interacting dimensions: the bodily, the mental, and the spiritual. To ignore the spiritual dimension of human well-being in the name of "science" is to miss that which makes us truly human. What is more, Frankl maintains that of the three dimensions of our being, it is the spiritual that most directly affects our health or illness, our sense of fulfillment or frustration. In contrast to those who focus on the bodily dimension of life and maintain that our primary motivational drive is the "will to pleasure," or those who emphasize the mental component and consequently argue for the "will to self-actualization," Frankl asserts that the "will-to-meaning" is the primary motivational drive in human life. Frankl's conception of psychological health thus differs from other systems of modern psychology

insofar as it considers man as a being whose main concern consists in fulfilling a meaning and in actualizing values, rather than in the mere gratification and satisfaction of drives and instincts, the mere reconciliation of the conflicting claims of id, ego and superego, or mere adaptation and adjustment to the society and environment.[18]

The types of frustrations and crises adults typically confront in midlife "do not emerge from conflicts between drives and instincts but rather from conflicts between various values; in other words, from moral conflicts or, to speak in a more general way, from spiritual problems."[19] The very essence of human life is the spiritual dynamic created by our fundamental responsibility for fulfilling a unique mission or vocation in life. To feel healthy and satisfied humans require not a tensionless state such as is produced by satiating our physical needs, but rather an active striving or struggling toward some worthy goal. The highest level of human fulfillment is produced within "a polar field of tension where one pole is represented by a meaning to be fulfilled and the other pole by the man who must fulfill it."[20]

According to Frankl, we can discover and achieve meanings in at least three different ways: (1) by creating values through active deeds; (2) by enduring suffering and thereby realizing an attitudinal achievement; and (3) by experiencing what he calls the Supra-Meaning of life through a prerational experience of an indwelling spiritual reality. The first of these is the most obvious. It refers to our ability to find meaning in our worldly accomplishments. By meeting the needs (whether those for food, friendship, or artistic enjoyment) of others we create meanings that have an existence and reality that live on even after our own death. That is, we find a meaning to our life by taking responsibility for making the world a better and more loving place for others.

One of Frankl's most original contributions to modern psychology was his perception of the meaning to be found even in moments of loss, grief, and pain. Much of life is beyond our control, thereby leaving our happiness at the mercy of outer conditions. There is, however, one aspect of life over which events in the outer environment have no power: the determination of what our attitude *toward* those events will be.

> Whenever one is confronted with an inescapable, unavoidable situation, whenever one has to face a fate that cannot be changed, e.g., an incurable disease, such as an inoperable cancer, just then is one given a last chance to actualize the highest value, to fulfill the deepest meaning, the meaning of suffering. For what matters above all is the attitude we take toward suffering, the attitude in which we take our suffering upon ourselves.[21]

Emphasizing that humanity's main concern is not to gain pleasure or to avoid pain, but rather to see a meaning in life, Frankl notes that it is often in moments of profound suffering that we can most readily assert our freedom to choose our attitude toward life and thereby achieve dignity and virtue in the face of tragedy. He tells, for example, of one of his patients who could not overcome the grief produced by the death of his wife. Frankl confronted this patient by asking him what would have happened had he died first, leaving his wife alone. The patient quickly realized that his wife would then have been the one to grieve and face loneliness and that the very event that caused his own suffering had spared her that torment. This realization alone gave his lonely life meaning. In other words, suffering ceases to be suffering the moment it finds a meaning (such as the meaning of making sacrifices for others or the meaning of building spiritual virtues amidst worldly adversity, etc.).

Both of these first two ways of fulfilling humanity's species-specific need for meaning can be considered as forms of what we have referred to as a "final" or attitudinal influence upon human well-being. What distinguishes Frankl's descriptions of psychological fulfillment is his argument that there is a deeper, more ultimate meaning to life that cannot itself be grasped by our finite intellectual capacities. He speaks of the existence of a "spiritual unconscious" that exists alongside our instinctual unconscious. The spiritual unconscious is the ultimate source of all environment-transcending activities such as art, love, and moral conscience. Our psyche, he explains, "reaches down into an unconscious ground," thereby making it possible for us to experience "a relationship between the immanent self and a transcendent thou."[22] According to Frankl humans can in this way avail themselves of the very *Logos* (i.e., divine plan or intrinsic structure) of life itself and in so doing lay hold of meanings that are in some fundamental way transcendent to the flux of everyday life.

It would appear, then, that many of the developmental tasks faced in adulthood "naturally" prompt individuals to grow in ways similar to those defined by James Fowler in his descriptions of faith development. The needs to sustain ethical commitment and find meanings that transcend the historical flux reveal certain limitations in what Fowler defined as "Stage Four" and "Stage Five" forms of faith-knowing. The quest for sustained fulfillment in adult life requires individuals to seek new forms of relationship to others, to themselves, and to that which is felt to be universal. The ideologically charged faith born of needs related to identity formation must give way to a faith capable of guiding the adult's need to discover new levels of meaning and new modes of feeling related to life. Shifts toward what Fowler calls "consolidative" and "universalizing" forms of faith-knowing characterize the cognitive transformations whereby mature adults reenvision their world in response to the midlife experiences

that disclose new and nonphysical dimensions to the environments
in which they move and have their being.

LIMITS AND ADULT DEVELOPMENT

Throughout the life cycle, human development consists of a continuous process whereby new personality strengths succeed upon
and grow out of older ones which are no longer capable of guiding the
individual to rewarding transactions with the larger environment.
Earlier in life, the ruptures or crises that elicit growth arise primarily
from the emergence of new organic potentials and a wider range of
interaction with the material, social, and economic worlds. Yet, as
life progresses, personal development is ever less an activity of ac-
commodating segments of reality presented to us through the socialization. Midlife presents us with an increasing number of developmental challenges that pertain to our mode of interacting with
realities that are not "out there" in any objective fashion. Facing the
irreversibility of our major decisions, asking such questions as Why
be moral? or Why live?, or questioning the meaning of any one chosen life, all confront us with the very limits of humanity's mental and
emotional resources for engaging life.

Each new stage in the course of personal growth represents the
equilibrated patterns of interaction between the individual organism and the wider environment. For this reason the study of "successful" human development has much light to shed on the larger
scientific and philosophical investigation of nature. That is, the
forms in which we best adapt to the environment reveal at least partial hints concerning the shape of that environment, of reality. Our
study has thus far already shown the great extent to which human fulfillment over the course of the life cycle is linked with the resolution
of developmental challenges which have a broadly religious or spiritual dimension to them. The claim being staked out here is that insofar as humans regularly and even predictably confront limit experiences, then one must also acknowledge that ego-dominated psychological processes cannot alone fully center the personality. The
implication is that the rhythms of the life cycle themselves prompt
the individual to search for a Self which in some fundamental way

transcends the historical flux. And, surely, this psychological observation must simultaneously have a great deal of ontological and metaphysical import. Among other things, it suggests that humans do inhabit environments that go beyond the physical world mediated by our sensory experience. And, of course, this is precisely the issue raised most poignantly in the prototypical limit experience—the confrontation of death in old age.

FOUR

AGING, DYING, AND INTEGRITY

By the latter stages of middle age, the shifting contours of the life cycle have already begun to favor those virtues or strengths that aim less at aligning the self with objective social structures than with some nonempirical reality. Individuals are, for example, gradually lured into valuing experience and wisdom more than physical prowess.[1] We also tend to shift from an orientation geared toward using persons to one of appreciating them. Third, we learn that if we are to prevent emotional impoverishment in face of the loss of loved ones we must remain flexible in building social relationships. And, finally, mental flexibility must persevere over and against closed-mindedness if we are to remain in the flow of life and avoid paths of stagnation.

The diminishment of physical abilities and shift in generational relationships, which occasioned midlife transformations, continue and even accelerate with the advancement of age. Eyesight, hearing, circulation, and digestion/elimination all commonly begin to atrophy. There is a marked increase in the incidence of incapacitating illnesses such as cancer, heart attacks, and strokes. So disproportionate are the physical assaults endured during the last years of life that for many, maintaining a sense of cohesiveness and wholeness becomes a primary struggle. And, too, as our seventies approach we find ourselves being displaced from the mainstream of business, social, and family life. We begin to acquire the status of "senior citizens," which is often a thinly veiled euphemism for "no longer socially needed." Whereas we once invested considerable amounts of time and planning to acquire worldly goods such as cars, homes, and furniture, old age requires that we learn to part with these.

Most persons living in modern American culture will undergo a series of moves whereby they relocate in smaller homes, apartments, and perhaps face extended stays in either a nursing home or hospital. Each successive move requires that we further detach ourselves from possessions and the memories they invoke.

Much of old age is spent in reminiscing about the past. Far from a sign of senility, as younger persons are prone to view it, reminiscence is a means of synthesizing past experiences in an attempt to reevaluate our lives and make appropriate value changes in an effort to adapt to new life circumstances.[2] As Erikson notes, integrity and wisdom in old age require the ability to see one's life whole and continue to affirm its meaning even in the face of its loss through death. The wisdom to differentiate between what truly matters and what is merely ornamental can only emerge from considerable amounts of retrospective analysis of one's supposed triumphs and defeats. For many, extended life review leads to an overriding sense of despair, depression, and related psychological disorders. But for others, reflection upon the relationship between the extrinsic features of one's own life and the intrinsic meanings of life itself gives rise to such personality achievements as candor, serenity, wisdom, and spiritual enlightenment.

The underlying theme of old age is, of course, prolonged reflection upon the reality and inevitability of one's own eventual death.[3] The earlier phases of adult life are past. Family and occupation have been given their full attention and have now been released. What seems obvious from a chronological point of view is not easily comprehended from an emotional or psychological point of view: Death is imminent and, with it, release from the human life cycle. As Freud so aptly described our difficulty in coming to terms with death:

> We were prepared to maintain that death was the necessary outcome of life. . . . In reality, however, we were accustomed to behave as if it were otherwise. We displayed an unmistakable tendency to "shelve" death,

to eliminate it from life. We tried to hush it up. . . . No-one believes in his own death. . . . In the unconscious everyone is convinced of his own immortality.[4]

Freud also recorded how one of his patients suffering from deep depression finally gained insight into the underlying cause of his anxiety. "Up till now," he confessed, "life has seemed an endless upward slope, with nothing but the distant horizon in view. Now suddenly I seem to have reached the crest of the hill, and there stretching ahead is the downward slope with the end of the road in sight . . . there is death observably present at the end."[5] Importantly, this insight was alone sufficient to enable that individual to take new and more fulfilling bearings on life. He began to acknowledge the stark fact that he would never achieve everything he was capable of desiring. Much would inevitably have to remain unfinished and unrealized. The integrity of his life would, in other words, depend not on the quantity of what he owned but on the quality of who he had been.

Old age and the approach of death complete the life cycle by bringing the individual back to the same developmental crisis confronted in infancy. Acquiring wisdom, as with basic trust, is not something that pertains to our physical or socioeconomic abilities. It is a fundamentally spiritual challenge in that it requires that we make a nonempirical judgment about the character of life and be capable of affirming its intrinsic goodness in spite of unavoidable pain and loss.

In sum, the quest to find integrity in our final years brings with it several new developmental challenges. These years demand that we detach ourselves from former work and family roles and instead seek out new lines of personality development. Aging also requires that we adopt new perspectives that avoid preoccupation with bodily ailments and relocate our identity in terms of what we have given, and continue to give, to others. And, finally, these years challenge us to learn ways of transcending self-preoccupation. As long as we identify only with the physical and social dimensions of selfhood, we remain vulnerable to continued assaults and loss. Yet by identifying with the various social and spiritual ways in which we live on beyond our physical lives, we can continue to greet life as fraught with opportunities for continued activity and growth.

ERIKSON AND THE LIFE CYCLE
COMPLETED

Each successive task that confronts us in life calls for, and hopefully elicits, new developmental strengths or virtues. If the demand for generativity can be considered the "ethical stage" in Erikson's model of normative psychological development, then the final stage might be called the "religious stage" in that it demands we confront and attempt to grow through a final limit to the life cycle.

Stage 8
Approximate Age: Old Age
Acquiring a Sense of Integrity
(and avoiding a sense of despair)
A Realization of Wisdom

As the adult works to assure a new generation of a trustworthy world, he or she gains a fuller perspective of his or her own cycle. This is the time for reflection, and for the enjoyment of grandchildren if there are any. This is a time for reflection, for reminiscing about one's life now viewed as a whole. Experiences are sifted through during daydreams and recollections. The individual is no longer caught up in the social games and popularity contests that absorbed so many of the early and middle years. Prestige, wealth, and power are no longer goals being sought but symbols of the many values clung to in the past, whether achieved or not. Life is consequently viewed less as a means toward socially defined ends, but as an end in itself.

Integrity emerges as a strength of personality insofar as the individual learns to look back on his or her life with satisfaction. Many, of course, look back upon their lives as a series of missed opportunities and missed directions; now in their twilight years they realize that it is too late to start over or undo the mistakes of the past. Wholeness and fulfillment in this stage require that we acquire a new perspective which can put these inevitable shortcomings in an appropriate context. Just as the acquisition of basic trust in life rests upon nonempirical judgments about the basic character of the universe, so does the acquisition of wisdom depend upon accepting life in its totality rather than its specifics. One cannot find integrity in one's own life unless the integrity of the whole of life can be affirmed. It is not the extrinsic utility of this or that thing we have done that is at stake, but whether there is any intrinsic meaning to the human enterprise itself. This is a religious rather than a scientific or ethical issue. As with all other limit experiences, this final developmental challenge clearly relativizes the scope and significance of human rationality. Logical analysis and scientific observation can guide us through many of the developmental challenges of the middle years, but they can tell us little about the intrinsic character or integrity of existence.

Integrity makes possible the virtue of wisdom. Wisdom is the concern with life itself in the face of death itself. Wisdom maintains and conveys the integrity of experience in spite of the decline of bodily and mental functions. It responds to the need of the oncoming generation for an integrated heritage and yet remains aware of the relativity of knowledge.

It is here that individuality finds its ultimate test, namely, our entrance into that region which we must enter alone. This is the "limit" of the human life cycle, the limit to the individual's continuance in the sequence of human generations. There are, of course, other "limit experiences" over the course of the life cycle (religious experiences, death of loved ones, profound guilt, deep moral reflection), but none has such the sting of finality or must be encountered while so alone. The religiosity of this stage must go well beyond the beliefs and doctrines of the churches because it must accept the doubts and frailties humans have when they so starkly face life's greatest trauma. Wisdom emerges as these doubts have been fully admitted and accepted even while continuing to affirm the intrinsic meaningfulness of life in all of its human ambiguities.

AGING AND THE FULFILLMENT OF LIFE

Erikson's assessment of the psychological themes of aging suggests that sustained vitality and fulfillment in old age is principally connected with one's perception of the *meaning* of who one has become and how one has cared for others.[6] In particular, it concerns one's confidence in whether that meaning is likely to be sustained in the face of physical decline and increasing closeness to death. As K. Brynoff Lyon points out in his theological appropriation of Erikson's work on aging, fulfillment in old age is the consummation of that primordial hope that marks the beginnings of life.[7] Integrity is impossible without a deeply rooted hope that who I have become and who I am now becoming can allow me to continue to realize values related to my sense of vitality up to, and inclusive of, my physical death.

Erikson well understands that this stage, as with all others, emerges not solely through self-initiated efforts but through the process of mutual activation whereby the environment inspires one with adaptive strengths even as we venture out in basic trust. The kind of integrity Erikson has in mind as commensurate to the limit dimension of human existence necessarily pertains to an environment that is transindividual and, for that matter, metaphysically transcendent. Erikson notes the ontological or metaphysical implications of humanity's experience of such "mutual activation" when confronted with the limits of our individual existence by obliquely suggesting that

> every human being's Integrity may be said to be religious (whether explicitly or not). Each person engages in an inner search for, and a wish to communicate with, that mysterious, that Ultimate Other: for there can be no "I" without an "Other" and no "We" without a shared "Other."[8]

Erikson's observations that the cardinal virtues of psychological health—hope and wisdom—are intimately connected with our search for the ultimate ground of our existence suggests that the process of aging may itself contain clues to the mystery of life. Even the very contemplation of old age exposes our basic attitudes toward life. Is old age a sad fate that should be acknowledged only when the signs can no longer be avoided? Do the elderly make us uncomfortable? Do we seek to avoid the elderly as much as possible? Do we fear the elderly partially because they remind us deep down of our own aging, our own inevitable destiny? It is precisely owing to the way in which old age raises these kinds of questions that it simultaneously promises to teach us so much. Because old age reveals both the dangers and the possibilities of the life span itself, it also points out the values and wisdom capable of enriching our younger years as well.

Most of us fear old age more than death itself. The prospect of undergoing a waning of strength, chronic illness and pain, prolonged hospitalization, or the possibility of poverty and despair gnaws at our confidence in what life has in store for us. In a society that idolizes youth, there is little room for the elderly. Contemporary Americans spend over five billion dollars a year on cosmetics that give the appearance of youth but only a small fraction of that to the the care of the elderly. The elderly are segregated from the mainstream of life in ways too numerous to describe. The media glorify youth in their news, commercials, and entertainment. As a society we overtly segregate the elderly by pushing them away from us through retirement, and by isolating them in nursing homes. Most find themselves unable to attend the kinds of events they formerly enjoyed due to poor lighting, the number of stairs to climb, lack of transportation, and so forth. In a more subtle or covert way we segregate the elderly from our lives by no longer sharing our lives with them. We conceal facts about our lives from them, thinking that they will be shocked. We no longer challenge their ideas or expect them to engage in lively give and take. The old are politely tolerated, but rarely taken seriously. They are accorded no prestige, no importance, no value in the overall functioning of society.

Compounding all of this is inevitable desolation as one's sphere of activity, love, and friendship slowly shrinks. With each passing year, ever more friends either move away or die, leaving us to face life increasingly alone. As Henri Nouwen and Walter Gaffney write in their *Aging: The Fulfillment of Life,* "You have only one life cycle to live and only a few really entered that cycle and became your travel companions, sharing the moments of ecstasy and despair, as well as the long days of routine living. When they leave you, you know you have to travel on alone. Even to the friendly people you will meet on your way, you will never be able to say, 'Do you remember?' because they were not there when you lived it. Then life becomes like a series of reflections in a broken window."[9] It is not simply that you now have less people with whom to share life, but that your personal history has been pillaged in such a way that even the fondest of memories can no longer glow as brightly. Rejected by society and stripped of our closest friends, we find that old age threatens to engulf us with bitterness and despair.

There are, however, values that if held fervently can help make aging a path toward continuing growth and fulfillment. Detachment, hope, humor, and, finally, vision are all revealed by the aging process as guides toward the achievement of integrity and wisdom in the face of experiences that might otherwise bring nothing but desolation and defeat.

Detachment refers to the steadfast refusal to confuse the quality of our being with the quantity of our having. Insofar as we view the meaning and purpose of our lives in economic or materialistic terms, old age will inevitably strip us of accustomed measures of self-worth. Age, for this reason, shows us the fallacy of attending only to the material surface of life. Throughout life we must learn to detach ourselves from material possessions, titles, and measures of success or status. If we do not, we forever remain at the mercy of outer conditions; we have no identity other than that given to us from without, thereby leaving our self-worth vulnerable to economic reversals, retirement, and the opinions of others. Detachment has been considered a spiritual virtue in nearly every world religion insofar as they maintain that the ultimate goal of life lies not in adapting ourselves to the social and economic environments but instead in preparing ourselves to experience divine spirit in a direct and mystical way. Hinduism, Buddhism, Judaism, Christianity, and Islam have all had followers who insist that our "highest" identity is not in the physical world but rather in a spiritual world or dimension that is found by turning one's identity inward toward nonphysical dimensions of life. Religions teach that only by first detaching ourselves from total identification with the physical can we become receptive to the inflow of the spiritual. And this, it seems, is also one of the lessons that the aging process reveals as well. If life is to continue to have meaning and purpose into old age, we must first acquire a sense of fundamental detachment from the material or physical. We must persistently refuse to attach any kind of ultimate significance to anything except our potential to become receptive to our inner spiritual depths. Detachment leads to wisdom in that it guides us toward life in a way that makes it possible to affirm life even in the face of physical loss or even death. By placing our identity in the spiritual rather than material aspects of life, it helps us approach any event—including the so-called terrible events such as a loss of a job, the death of a loved one, or a serious illness—as an opportunity for continued growth and development.

Hope follows from detachment. That is, hope is very different from wishing in that wishing has to do with the desire for specific physical possessions or social status. In contrast, hope has to do with sustaining a basic trust in life, as Erikson noted when he made it the foundational virtue of a fulfilling life cycle. Hope imparts the emotional strength and desire to look forward continually to life even when those things we have wished for (e.g., continuous health for ourselves and loved ones, money, prestige) have not come our way. Hope makes us willing to start anew after reversals. By giving us an assurance of life's fundamentally trustworthy character despite the many adversities we have faced, hope enables us to seek out new opportunities, redefine our goals, change directions, and find integrity even amidst loss. Hope is, of course, fueled by religious faith and its affirmation that all is not vanity. Religious faith makes hope possible by imparting confidence that there is a will or power central to the universe that is receptive toward our efforts and will, in the end, bestow wholeness upon our lives.

Humor, too, is a psychological or attitudinal factor capable of helping us preserve integrity amidst loss. It relativizes the seriousness of our predicaments by letting us for an instant glimpse our lives from another perspective, in which no physical event can be taken as devastating or final. In this way humor promotes detachment. Humor helps us not to take the degree of success or failure too seriously but rather to measure our lives in terms of the attitudes we take toward the outer world. Humor is an achievement of will and spirit; it signals the individual's ability to see the meaning of his or her life in ways that transcend its physical appearance and thus makes possible the serenity of wisdom.

Old age also prompts the development of a type of vision that can lead us beyond the limit or boundary of the finite self and disclose a supersensible reality that envelops or surrounds the physical. Vision of this sort shifts the focus of our identity away from the material to the spiritual, from the physical to the metaphysical, and from the finite to the infinite. In this way it sustains hope in the future, even when that future contains the dissolution of the physical body. And, as Nouwen and Gaffney have observed, this vision gradually "invites us to a total, selfless surrender in which the distinction between life and death slowly loses its pain."[10] The vision potentially developed in old age closely resembles the vision born of mystical experience in that both reveal that the purpose of human existence is to draw ever closer toward the divine light. Memories, regrets, and fear dissolve as the self becomes enveloped by a sense of pure light and pure love. A Dutch priest named Han Fortmann expressed the dawn of this life-enriching vision when on his deathbed he wrote,

> I proceed from the simple irrefutable fact that in the crucial moments of life . . . (such as death), even though people come from diverging cultures and religions, they find that same essential word: Light! For isn't it true? There must be a basic similarity between the Enlightenment spoken of by the Hindus and Buddhists and the Eternal Light of the Christians. Both die into the Light. One practical could well be that the Buddhist, more than the contemporary Christian, has learned to live with the light (nirvana) as a reality long before he dies. . . . That interior participation, that Enlightenment, intended "for every man who comes into the world"—as John's gospel puts it—has received far less attention in practical preaching than in the teaching of Satori in Zen Buddhism or Samadi in Hinduism. But whoever has once met God no longer finds the hereafter question interpreting. Whoever has learned to live in the Great Light is no longer worried by the problem of whether the Light will still be there tomorrow. . . . The need to pose skeptical questions about the hereafter seems to disappear as the divine Light again becomes a reality in everyday life, as it is meant to, of course, in all religions.[11]

These words give poignancy to the religious character of aging and the virtue of Wisdom that makes it possible to sustain hope even in the face of death. The kind of vision that makes aging a path toward continued growth reveals that our physical life and world are but part of a wider spiritual environment; it imparts a confidence that what, from the physical perspective, would appear to be the loss of life is, from the spiritual perspective, but one more cycle of regeneration and rebirth whereby a new dimension arises from and succeeds upon an earlier dimension. Just as in our planet's evolutionary history each new dimension of life (i.e., mineral, organic, animal, human) grows out of and displays developmental growth over and beyond its predecessors, so does religious vision show physical death to be but a transition to a dimension in which continued growth toward the light will be possible without further restriction by a now weary physical body. And thus what first appeared to be an ever-restricting path is transformed by religious vision into an avenue of ever-widening life. The wisdom born of a vision of the light is the principal lesson or teaching that religion can offer to an understanding of a life cycle optimally adapted to our repeated encounters with the limit dimension of human existence. This is, for example, undoubtedly the reason for the enduring appeal of the last several books in the Old Testament, or Jewish sacred writings. The biblical books of Job, Proverbs, and Ecclesiastes are usually referred to as "wisdom literature" in that rather than claiming origin in a distinct act of supernatural revelation such as that delivered to Moses on Mt. Sinai, they are instead decidedly humanistic. They offer not holy truths delivered from above, but sincere—even skeptical—human inquiries into the meaning and nature of human existence. They draw their content from daily life and are, in fact, full of jokes, riddles, and sexual frankness. Their common purpose is to depict the character traits most conducive to human happiness and thereby to transmit the accumulated wisdom of one generation to the next such that it might benefit from the experiences and mistakes of those who have gone before them. When they offer counsel (e.g., avoiding drinking to excess or not committing adultery), they do so not by referring to some divine decree but by pointing out the long-term consequences of various courses of action. For the most part, all three of these books represent a heightened degree of religious doubt and cynicism. They were written by individuals who saw the doctrinal formulations of a second-hand faith crumble under the weight of skeptical reason and repeated observation of life's tragedies. Yet all three eventually endorse religious faith by appealing to its pragmatic truths in terms of enriching the human enterprise. In so doing they force us to reflect upon our lives in ways that will "naturally" lead us to frame our identities, goals, and ambitions in terms of both a religious tradition and a living community.

An even clearer example of a religion's attempt to help each new generation acquire the wisdom of spiritual vision is that of Hinduism's concept of the four stages of life. The Hindu faith maintains that each of us has certain duties or obligations (*dharma*) that must be performed to keep our lives in harmony with the lawful structure by which divine spirit maintains the universe. To best adapt to this underlying pattern of the universe, we are counseled to structure our lives into four quite distinct stages or phases. The first of these is the stage of being a student. During this stage of life our primary responsibility is that of acquiring all the knowledge that previous generations have accumulated. A sacred ceremony marks entrance into the stage of studentship to impress upon the young their solemn responsibility to store away as much knowledge and as many insights as possible. Students had few immediate responsibilities to society; these would come in due time. Rather, as a student one must cultivate habits, develop character, and study deeply the culture's sacred scriptures such that their insights will be fully internalized to be called upon as needed later in life.

The second stage of the ideal Hindu life cycle is that of the householder. As the name indicates, this is the stage marking one's adult existence as spouse, parent, neighbor, and citizen. With our physical and mental powers fully developed, this is the stage in which our interests are naturally directed outward. The stage begins with marriage and is subsequently followed by the duties required by family, vocation, and community. This is, incidentally, the moral stage of life in that one's life is primarily structured by the many responsibilities imposed upon us by religious and social expectations. It is expected that during this, the longest, stage of life we will rightfully wish to pursue the goals of both pleasure (including sex and other sensual delights) and material wealth. These, Hinduism tells us, are not only natural but indispensable parts of the overall spiritual pattern of life. Provided that both pleasure and wealth are sought in ways that respect the basic moral fabric of community life, they are to be pursued and enjoyed to the fullest. Yet, says Hinduism, seasons of life come and go. It is proper that as our duties as parent and householder come to end we seek a new identity befitting our new stage in life.

Hindu scripture advises that when our hair begins to turn gray, our skin begins to wrinkle, and we find that our children are off and on their own, it is time to enter the third stage of the life cycle. The third stage might be called that of retirement, though it intends not only retiring from our worldly vocation but detaching ourselves from life in general. After all, *if* there is no more to life than what is perceived by the physical senses, then our last years should be fraught with despair and regret. *But,* if there are dimensions of the self and the universe that transcend the physical, then there is the promise of spiritual discovery and the beginning of a shift in identity toward that aspect of the self that does not die when the body dies but rather continues on to a new round of growth, learning, and development. This stage requires withdrawal from the hustle-bustle of everyday life. We are counseled to take temporary leave of our families and neighbors and, accompanied by no one other than our spouse, live alone for a period of time sufficient to turn attention away from worldly preoccupations. This should be a stage filled with prayer, meditation, introspection, and the reading of religious literature. The purpose is to move our attention behind the world's facade and to obtain union with the universal spirit that permeates the cosmos in its every detail.

The fourth and final stage of life differs from the third only in degree. This is the stage that Hindu scriptures describe as living wholly "identified with the eternal Self and beholding nothing else." We have attended to the lessons and duties of this life. Future spiritual development awaits our transition out of the present earthly body and into a new set of learning opportunities (whether in a future life on earth as the Hindu doctrine of reincarnation suggests or in a bodiless spiritual dimension as the Hindu doctrine of salvation describes). Individuals in this stage are sufficiently proficient in meditation that they have been afforded direct experiential awareness that the true self is neither physical nor mental, but spiritual. With this saving vision they approach each day concerned not for self-aggrandizement, but for continued spiritual purification and enlightenment. Detached from the worldly concerns that rightfully preoccupied them during earlier stages, they now live in and for spiritual vision. As Hindu scripture says of the individual in this stage:

> By deep meditation let him recognize the subtle nature of [divine spirit] and its presence in all organisms. . . . He who has in this manner gradually given up all attachments reposes in God alone. . . . He attains the eternal God.

CONFRONTING DEATH AND DYING

No individual has done more to draw modern Americans' attention to the personal experience of dying than Elisabeth Kubler-Ross. When Kubler-Ross began lecturing on the psychological aspects of dying during the 1960s she found herself a lone voice in a society that she came to label a "death-denying society." The cult of youth projected by the media banishes the topics of aging and death from our awareness. Worse yet, contemporary obsessions with youth and beauty make dying appear somehow unnatural or possibly even avoidable. And, too, we are increasingly insulated from the experience of dying. Whereas fifty years ago most people died in the familiar surroundings of home and family, today more than half of all deaths occur in hospital rooms to persons who have been so heavily sedated as to be incapable of consciously sharing or experiencing this final phase of their life cycle. Even the medical community has lost any sense for what life or death might mean. Trained as technicians of scientific medicine, doctors and nurses have never really thought about how one might define life or attend to an individual who is in the final stages of reflecting upon what his or her life was all about.

Kubler-Ross's study of the dying process began by accident. A group of theology students came to her to ask for her assistance in writing a paper on a crisis in human experience. Having chosen death as the biggest crisis a human ever has to face, they were at a loss as to how they might study this fundamental human phenomenon. She promised them that she would help them interview dying patients at the University of Chicago hospital where she worked. After an awkward beginning, Kubler-Ross realized that the dying have a great deal to teach us. Over the next few years she conducted extensive interviews with over four hundred patients. She found that most wanted to talk and very much wished to have someone share their thoughts and feelings. Sadly enough, most of these patients had found that their families, physicians, and even ministers were so uncomfortable about facing up to the reality of death that no one had ever been willing to simply sit and listen to them. Given the opportunity, these patients responded as though Kubler-Ross had opened a floodgate. They shared with her feelings, reactions, fears, and hopes that had obsessed them since becoming aware of their imminent death. Sorting through these interviews, Kubler-Ross began to detect a fairly predictable sequence or pattern in the dying process.[12] She has concluded that patients typically go through five distinct stages between their initial awareness of terminal illness and the moment of their death. These five stages highlight the attitudinal or value

adjustments that tend to emerge amidst our confrontation with the
ultimate limit of the life cycle.

According to Kubler-Ross the first stage of the dying process is
that of denial. Most patients respond to being told that they are
terminally ill with shock and disbelief. Surely there has been a mis-
take. Perhaps the X-rays were mixed up or the laboratory technician
did not follow the proper procedures. Denials of this sort last any-
where from a few minutes to a few months. Few patients maintain
this denial to the very end. Most gradually begin to see that they are
seriously ill and recognize that things are not as usual. Denial does,
however, serve a psychologically important function in that it provides an emotional buffer against shock. Many of those who remain
in the stage of shock for an extended period turn to religion as a
means of not coming to rational terms with their approaching death.
Religion for these individuals becomes a form of wish fulfillment; it
promises the possibility of a faith healing or the ability to petition
God through prayer. This is a tricky subject because surely the pages
of human history are filled with cures that have seemingly miracu-
lous elements to them. But in the majority of cases, the type of religion most commonly seen in this stage is that of self-serving petitions
to a supreme being and tends to dissipate as awareness of the inevitability of death sets in.

The second stage is that of anger. When patients cannot maintain
their denial any more, they begin to feel intense amounts of rage, resentment, envy. Why me? What have I done to deserve this? I have so
much still to do, so many depend upon me! It isn't fair! This rage is
often taken out on close family members or the hospital staff. The patient becomes nasty, demanding, criticizing, and harsh. Some patients vent this anger toward God: Why did you let this happen to
me? What kind of a God would torment me and my family this way?
The challenge to faith presented by one's own approaching death
causes many to begin questioning their religious beliefs for what is
often the first time in their lives. Because questions concerning the
nature and meaning of life are now raised in the most radical way, individuals are potentially drawn beyond the perspective of their own
finite ego to some transpersonal point of view. And thus, for many,
the encounter with death initiates a transition between a secondhand
religious faith and one that is appropriated as a firsthand, living

reality. Kubler-Ross relates the experience of a nun who was hospi-
talized for a terminal illness. Placed in a room with another dying patient who became increasingly cynical and bitter about religion, this
nun for the first time took seriously the doubts humans might legiti-
mately have about God. Initially thrown out of her accustomed equilibrium, she gradually realized that it was precisely from this other
patient's anger, resentment, and cynicism that

> I actually got my faith. Really, it's my own faith now. And it's faith, it
> isn't theory of someone else, meaning I don't understand God's way and
> many things that happen, but I believe that God is greater than I am and
> when I look at the young people dying, and their parents, and everyone
> says what a waste and that, I can see. I say, "God is love," and I mean it
> now. It isn't words, I really mean it.[13]

The third stage is that of bargaining. In the bargaining stage people
begin to pray for another year to live; they promise to attend church
every week if they are granted a bit more time to live; they pledge to
become missionaries or donate money to charity. In nearly every
case these bargains are made with God. Insofar as these bargains
continue to serve the individual's own interests, they reflect a fairly
immature and superstitious form of religious thought.

As the inevitability of death becomes unescapable, patients enter
into a stage of depression. He or she becomes overwhelmed by a
sense of utter loss. Most of us have experienced the grief and despair
that comes from losing a loved one. Imagine, then, the depression
that comes from losing not one person, but everybody you have ever
known or loved. The individual in this stage acknowledges that she
or he is facing a final separation from life. What is more, his or her
death will adversely affect a good many others. Mounting medical
bills, unpaid family expenses, the loss of a family breadwinner, and
so forth, all become stark realities. For this reason Kubler-Ross distinguishes between what she calls reactive depression and preparatory depression. Reactive depression emerges from the patient's
anxieties over the side effects of his or her death: financial burdens,
the impact upon his or her children, and so forth. Most of these can
be alleviated by help and assistance from others. Preparatory grief,
on the other hand, must be undergone alone. This grief pertains to
one's preparations to detach ourselves from life and is a necessary
step toward the final acceptance of death. The patient must begin to

separate himself or herself from the people he or she will be leaving in the near future. All that others can do is sit beside them, touch them, and be empathetic listeners. Words become empty at a time like this and it does no good to try to cheer them up as this would only divert them from the reality of the situation and the necessary task at hand.

The final stage in Kubler-Ross's model of the dying process is that of acceptance. She is careful to point out that this stage should not be misunderstood as a period of happiness or joy. It is, rather, a stage of cool detachment during which patients begin to separate; when they no longer wish to talk; when they view their life business as finished; and when they simply want the silent companionship of someone with whom they can feel comfortable. Acceptance of death is synonymous with what Erikson called the sense of integrity or wisdom with which we can continue to affirm the meaning of life even in the face of its personal loss. Those of Kubler-Ross's patients who achieved this final stage reveal two somewhat different paths whereby death might be robbed of its sting and accepted as somehow a clue to life's mysteries. The first has to do with finding integrity in one's completed life tasks. Patients who can look back over their lives and confidently affirm that they have contributed to the well-being of others find consolation even in death. They know that they have contributed to the sequence of generations and thereby rest content with the dignity of having given back to life all that they have taken from it.

Whereas the first path toward acceptance is essentially humanistic in that it pertains only to our concrete actions toward other persons, the second is frankly spiritual or metaphysical in nature. Kubler-Ross found that those rare individuals who have an "intrinsic faith" readily find acceptance of death. Her interviews reveal that some individuals find the wisdom to accept death long before they approach serious illness. Having developed a firsthand faith, they had long ago come to identify themselves not as a body who possesses a soul, but rather as a soul who possesses a body. Acceptance of death, then, is the byproduct of a vision of the light. Insofar as we come to place our primary identity in some spiritual or nonphysical aspect of our being, death need no longer be viewed as a final barrier. Indeed, death can actually be viewed as a type of healing in that it alone makes possible a release from a no longer useful body. In other words, death confronts individuals in such a way as to disclose a limit dimension to human life that can best be resolved by learning to affirm and identify with some supersensible reality beyond the limits of our finite personalities.

BEYOND THE LIFE CYCLE?

The question of immortality has long puzzled the human mind. Conclusive arguments elude philosophical analysis. Yet from time to time individuals have pointed to certain types of "empirical evidence" in support of their belief that the human life cycle is but a chapter in the history of the soul. Spiritualists, for example, claim that they offer empirical proof of life after death. In fact, nearly every culture, both modern and ancient, has produced individuals who claim that they can communicate with departed souls by entering into some type of altered state of consciousness or by using some special device such as a ouija board. Testimonies concerning ghosts, poltergeists, and spirit possession abound in the folklore of every civilization.

Our era has produced its own efforts to establish the existence of an afterlife on the basis of "empirical data" said to be commonly recurring features of the life cycle. In the early 1970s Raymond Moody began collecting accounts of strange experiences reported by people who had come close to dying.[14] After interviewing 150 individuals who had undergone "clinical death," he began to discover recurring patterns in the near-death experience. A near-death experience has an ineffable quality about it, somehow defying reduction to ordinary language; it is accompanied by feelings of peace and quiet; there is often the experience of the mind or psyche separating from the physical body (what is called an "out-of-the-body experience"), during which the individual can look back down on himself or herself as though witnessing the whole scene from the air; this is usually followed by an experience of traveling down a dark tunnel and at the end meeting a "Being of Light" variously interpreted as God, Christ, or angelic beings; the individual usually claims to see and meet the spirit-bodies of close friends and neighbors; they experience a moment of startling intensity during which the "being of light" presents to them a panoramic review of their life; individuals then seem to approach a border or limit at which point they for some reason begin to "come back" to their physical body and gradually regain their physical vital signs and consciousness. Moody found that subjects who had a near-death experience were affected in several ways. They lost all fear of death and instead described it as a condition of extraordinary beauty and peace. They came to view life as a precious gift and became much more loving and considerate of others. And finally, they became interested in seeking ever more knowledge about life and in investigating the ultimate philosophical questions about the nature and meaning of life.

Moody acknowledged that his findings did not constitute a scientific study in that they were based on patients' own accounts and were thus not produced under controlled conditions of any kind. Nor did his accumulated data conclusively prove that there is life after death in that all of these individuals had obviously not died, but had merely come close to death. Yet clearly Moody himself found the consistency or uniformity of his subjects' reported experiences compelling evidence of the existence of a postphysical plane of reality. Moody tried to support his personal belief in the validity of his data by showing how clearly they are paralleled in many biblical passages, the writings of Plato, various mystical texts, and, most important, in *The Tibetan Book of the Dead,* which records the experiences of individuals adept at entering deep meditational trances and who claim to have temporarily transcended the physical plane and glimpsed the spiritual dimension into which the soul will travel upon its release from the physical body at the moment of death. Moody further believes that additional research into the subject of near-death experiences will not only contribute to our conceptions of the afterlife, but will also shed light on the real meaning and purpose of our current physical lives. It is probable, he suggested, that "we cannot fully understand this life until we catch a glimpse of what lies beyond it."[15]

Michael Sabom, a surgeon, set out to subject Moody's findings to more systematic investigation and scrutiny. Originally skeptical of Moody's claims, Sabom soon found that about 40 percent of all surgical patients who had come close to dying could consciously remember and report undergoing a near-death experience almost exactly like those Moody reported.[16] Sabom's subjects described having experienced a sense of timelessness followed by a separation from their physical bodies. Not only did they report looking down and watching their bodies being operated on from above, but many claimed to have traveled clairvoyantly to other locations during their out-of-the-body experience. And, too, most encountered either a "Light" or a "being of light" from which they received assurance of their well-being. Interestingly, Sabom's subjects usually recounted what he terms a "life review" during which their entire lives from childhood on flashed panoramically through their consciousness. Invariably they would begin to see that they still had "work" yet to do in their lives and, upon returning to waking consciousness from their brush with death, felt that they had an intensified interest in developing loving and caring human relationships.

Because of the more controlled way in which Sabom set about getting his data, he could assess the significance of these findings more systematically than had Moody. For example, Sabom claimed that his subjects' experiences could not possibly have been mere hallucinations since they offered vivid descriptions of events that had transpired in the operating rooms and that were verified as accurate in every detail. And, too, he could eliminate the possibility that these descriptions of the operation came from perceptions during the semiconscious condition produced by anesthetics because they could not possibly have come from someone lying on the operating table. In several instances patients offered accurate accounts of procedures that Sabom concludes could only have been observed by the patients from above the operating table, as indeed they claimed they were in an out-of-the-body condition. Sabom is personally convinced that his research on near-death experiences establishes the empirical reality of a spiritual dimension of life that exists independently of the space/time physical world.

Kenneth Ring, a university psychologist who collaborated with Sabom as part of his own extensive studies of near-death experiences, likewise believes that the data support the theory that human nature overlaps with a wider spiritual universe.[17] Not only did Ring's research corroborate the major features of both Moody's and Sabom's findings, but he also discards possible neurological efforts to explain these findings (e.g., the argument that the nervous system produces these symptoms as a type of hallucination when in a state of severe shock) and suggests instead that Western scientists take seriously the beliefs found in many Eastern religions that have for centuries maintained that the human self is composed simultaneously of three bodies: the physical, the astral (which can be likened to the concept of the soul), and the causal (which can be likened to the Christian concept of spirit). Ring argues that this metaphysical interpretation of the human self offers an appropriate framework within which to explain near-death experiences.

> If our consciousness actually operates through *three* bodies—rather than just "in" the physical part of our being—then obviously the death of the physical body, rather than annihilating consciousness, *frees* it. Following [this] formulation, the out-of-body experience which occurs near death is actually a state of affairs where one's consciousness is functioning fully in the astral body. The clarity of perception and lucidity of mind commonly reported in this state is a consequence of one's consciousness being freed of the "drag" of the physical body. . . . The encounter with a "presence" or a "being of light" and the entrance into a "higher world" also are facets of the [near-death experience] which are easy to account for within [this] framework. Each of the three bodies is said to be sensitive to a different energy domain. The physical body is of course responsive to the physical world to which its sensory systems are "naturally" suited. The astral body (and similarly the causal body) is attuned to another (but penetrating) energy domain, usually said to be of "higher frequencies." When one is functioning in one's astral body, therefore, one becomes sensitive to the things of that world (or domain).[18]

Ring openly admits that most persons will find his interpretations preposterous; he merely suggests that his critics return to the actual empirical data furnished by individuals who have had a near-death experience and attempt to formulate a theory that can handle the evidence as cogently.

Kubler-Ross, for one, has long wrestled with near-death phenomena and has arrived at conclusions strikingly similar to Sabom's and Ring's. Kubler-Ross has been impressed by patients' repeated testimonies of undergoing an out-of-the-body experience during which they experience a world of supernatural beauty and are greeted by someone on "the other side." Going well beyond any claims made by Moody, Sabom, or Ring, Kubler-Ross believes she has to have been visited by departed spirits who have materialized their spirit bodies in order to meet with her and convince her of the reality of life after death. These spirits convinced her of the importance of viewing human existence as a type of school whose purpose is to present souls with continuous opportunities to develop and grow.[19] Kubler-Ross believes that in her studies of death she has found life. She says, "Death does not really exist. Death is simply a shedding of the physical body. And I do not just believe that. I *know* that. To me this is a very big difference. . . . This work with dying patients has helped me to find my own religious identity, to know that there is life after death and to know that we will be reborn again one day in order to complete the tasks we have not been able or willing to complete in this lifetime. It is in this context that I also begin to see the meaning of suffering and understand why even children have to die."[20]

Research on near-death experiences does not, of course, offer anything in the way of conclusive proof concerning either the existence or nature of the afterlife. This research only consists of the verbal reports of individuals who have come near dying (and who by definition have not died). Their reports undoubtedly reflect their cultural conditioning and pre-expectations. They could also be accounted for in terms of the electrochemical activity of the brain under conditions of extreme shock. Yet whatever else we make of these and other such efforts to speak of that which lies beyond the "limits" of human life, it is at least important to realize that human nature often seems to point beyond itself. Any empirical account of the human condition must acknowledge the repeated occurrence of experiences that offer individuals subjectively compelling insights into the limit dimension of existence. On empirical grounds alone it is only fitting that we turn to these experiences in order to find important clues concerning the nature and function of religion over the course of the life cycle.

FIVE

RELIGION AND SELF-TRANSCENDENCE

This book is concerned with how we should go about viewing human fulfillment, the meaning of life, and the values and/or personality traits that can best orient us to the widest range of satisfactions. The general thesis being advanced is that it is impossible to consider the life span in its entirety without recognizing the religious character of many of life's most profound challenges. Thus far we have examined numerous experiences that confront individuals with an ultimate limit to their existence and in so doing induce them to take what might be defined as a broadly religious or spiritual attitude toward life. There are, in other words, aspects of common human experience that cause us to "bump" into the limits of our rational comprehension of life and thereby set us searching for that which lies beyond the boundaries of finite existence.

There is, however, another kind of limit experience in which we do not so much bump into the limitations of human existence as find ourselves suddenly beyond them. What we variously call mystical insights, aesthetic delight, conversion experiences, intense joy, creativity, unconditional love, or religious ecstasy are all moments in which we unexpectedly find ourselves in the presence of a More which transforms our very life. Such moments imbue everyday life with a new vitality and richness. They revitalize us and become the nucleus of a new way of interpreting life. Limit experiences of this expansive sort teach us that we are somehow enveloped by a "higher reality" and that it is from this higher reality that our lives derive their highest happiness and good.

GLIMPSING THE SACRED IN "PEAK EXPERIENCES"

Writing during the 1960s and 70s, the psychologist Abraham Maslow expressed his dissatisfaction with both the scientific and religious thinking found in contemporary America. Science, he claimed, had become so dominated by the experimental method that it could no longer study those aspects of human nature that cannot be measured or quantified. The scientific study of human behavior has simply ignored such concepts as creativity, love, freedom, and playfulness and instead concentrates only on what can be explained according to the machinelike responses observed in laboratory experiments with animals. In Maslow's view, the worst culprit of this modern tendency to reduce human nature to the fixed determinisms of both our biological nature and social conditioning is psychology. Behavioral psychologists base their theories of human nature on the conditioned behavior of rats and monkeys; psychoanalytic psychologists use their observations of mentally and emotionally disturbed patients. Lost in our modern culture is any recognition of what characterizes human nature when it is at its healthiest, most creative, most fully developed, most free from environmental conditioning.

Maslow charged that our major religious traditions have done little more than modern science to give us a vision of humanity's highest potentials. Maslow was fully committed to modern intellectual thought (e.g., the findings of comparative religion, biblical scholarship, evolutionary science, the empirical method of discovering truth, etc.) and thus found our culture's dominant religious institutions incapable of offering authoritative accounts of the highest levels of human development. Maslow further criticized organized religion for turning spirituality into a set of habits, behaviors, dogmas, and rituals which have become so empty as to be antireligious. That is, the repetition of ritualized behaviors and the recitation of legalistic doctrines so dominate organized religions that their members lose or forget the subjectively religious experience which alone opens individuals to the reality of the transcendent or spiritual.

Maslow's intention was to enlarge the scope of psychological science to include the types of experiences traditionally associated with religion. A suitably enlarged science, he maintained, can accommodate the data of mystical consciousness and self-transcendence and thereby allow us to study humanity's higher nature empirically. He believed that his own research on the psychological phenomenon of self-actualization offered an important first step in this direction. Maslow recognized that if psychology was to develop a more complete and comprehensive science of the human person, it would have to begin by studying people who had realized their potentialities to the fullest. He therefore undertook an intensive investigation of individuals who could safely be characterized as creative and self-directing individuals. Using both living subjects and biographical information about individuals such as Lincoln, Jefferson, Beethoven, Walt Whitman, and Thoreau, Maslow began to discover a number of characteristics that distinguished these self-actualizing persons from others: (1) they have an air of detachment and a need for privacy; (2) they accept themselves and others for who they are; (3) they are problem-centered rather than self-centered; (4) they are extremely energetic and spontaneous; (5) they perceive life in fresh rather than stereotyped ways; (6) they are able to identify with all of humanity; (7) they resist conformity to the culture and transcend the environment rather than mindlessly responding to it; (8) most report having had profound mystical or spiritual experiences, though not necessarily interpreted in conventional religious terms.[1]

The last of these, the recurrence of mystical or spiritual experiences among self-actualizing persons, came to dominate Maslow's research and theoretical interests. Although he at first thought that such experiences were rare phenomena, he soon discovered that nearly every person has such moments of emotional intensity in which they come to feel fully integrated and spontaneous. Maslow put the label of "peak experiences" on those moments in which a person's talents and powers come together in a particularly efficient and intensely enjoyable way. Defined this way, peak experiences are episodes or emotional spurts that occur in the midst of creative activities, interpersonal relationships, and the accomplishment of tasks.

Peak experiences impart the sense of expressiveness, the feeling of being in perfect harmony with the whole of reality, and a long-lasting conviction that life has a higher meaning and that we somehow contribute to its realization. Peak experiences are, in this sense, therapeutic. They give us a vivid feeling of being whole, integrated, and having a place in the greater scheme of things. They enable us to feel no longer controlled by the outer environment, but rather capable of free and creative activity.

Maslow observed that during a peak experience individuals undergo a pronounced transformation. It is as though they temporarily transcend the psychological activities associated with development or becoming and find themselves participating directly in Being. Instead of feeling themselves to be adapting to the extrinsic features of their physical and social environments, they feel as though they have momentarily united with life's intrinsic meanings and structures. Maslow writes that peak experiences not only impart the feeling of existing beyond time and space, but they appear "as if they were perceptions of a reality independent of man and persisting beyond his life."[2] Peak experiences are for this reason almost prototypes of humanity's natural religiousness—that is, religious experience occurring independently of organized religious institutions and interpreted without reference to revealed scriptures. Maslow maintained that peak experiences evidence

> practically everything that, for example, Rudolf Otto defines as characteristic of the religious experience—the holy; the sacred; creature feeling; humility; gratitude and oblation; thanksgiving; awe before the *mysterium tremendum;* the sense of the divine, the ineffable; the sense of littleness before mystery; the quality of exaltedness and sublimity; the awareness of limits and even of powerlessness; the impulse to surrender and to kneel; a sense of the eternal and of the fusion with the whole of the universe . . . [3]

One of the primary consequences or effects of having a peak experience is that it provides what Maslow describes as an "acute identity-experience." Persons in peak experiences feel more integrated, unified, whole, and of-a-piece. They feel at the peak of their powers and hence more spontaneous and expressive. They also become more loving and accepting since they are more capable of transcending their ego and perceiving others without the usual gloss of self-interest.

The kinds of learnings and transformations that are engendered by peak experiences have an importance or validity that Maslow believes is ordinarily missed by modern academic psychology. Peak experiences do not make four apples visible where there were only three before; nor do the apples suddenly change into bananas. The revelatory character of peak experiences comes from the way in which they produce a shift in attention, a change in the way we organize our perceptions and differentiate between important and trivial aspects of experience. Peak experiences transform our approach to the interpretation of life such that we recognize that "the sacred is *in* the ordinary, that it is to be found in one's daily life, in one's neighbors, friends and family."[4] Peak experiences teach us to glimpse the sacred in and through the momentary, the worldly. They convince us that our world of becoming is enveloped by a world of Being from which it receives its wholeness, creativity, and meaning. As Maslow puts it, "Anyone who cannot perceive the sacred, the eternal, the symbolic, is simply blind to an aspect of reality. . . . The conception of heaven that emerges from the peak-experiences is one which exists all the time all around us, always available to step into for a little while at least."[5]

Maslow believed that his studies of peak experiences furnished the foundations for a synthesis of religious and psychological perspectives of human nature. By showing how spiritual values and experiences have a naturalistic meaning, Maslow believed that he had simultaneously pointed the way for an enlarged science and an empirically grounded religion. He pointed out that many leading theologians of the twentieth century already agree that God should be defined

> not as a person, but as a force, a principle, a gestalt-quality of the whole of Being, an integrating power that expresses the unity and therefore the meaningfulness of the cosmos, the "dimension of depth," etc. At the same time, scientists are increasingly giving up the notion of the cosmos as a kind of simple machine. . . . These two groups (sophisticated theologians and sophisticated scientists) seem to be coming closer and closer together in their conception of the universe as having some kind of unity

and integration, as growing and evolving and having direction and, therefore, having some kind of "meaning."[6] According to Maslow, the scientific study of the farthest reaches of human nature reveals the purely secularist point of view to be incomplete. Humanity, at its most developed and creative moments, manifests a higher and transcendent nature that in some fundamental way stands "beyond" the developmental stages of the life cycle. Maslow's observations here implicitly qualify or relativize the whole life cycle approach to human religiosity. The central "message" of religious experience would appear to be that human becoming is in some fundamental way transcended by an ontologically higher dimension of Being. Himself committed to the importance of the developmental process, Maslow admitted a paradox in his work: "The goal of identity (self-actualization, autonomy, individuation, Horney's real self, authenticity, etc.) seems to be simultaneously an end-goal in itself, and also a transitional goal, a rite of passage, a step along the path to the transcendence of identity."[7] It was Maslow's conviction that the peak experiences he studied revealed that the realm of becoming is somehow related to, participates in, and even contributes to the realm of Being.[8]

The significance of Maslow's studies is that they highlight the psychological influences exerted by those types of religious experience that conform to his description of peak experiences. Religious experience potentially transforms an individual's psychological constitution in clearly identifiable ways. It enables individuals to transcend environmental conditionings and instead respond to life from the felt-sense of a "higher" set of meanings and purposes. For this reason religious experiences impart a kind of peace, spiritedness, and heightened sense of self-worth that can be acquired in almost no other way.

CONVERSION AND SELF-UNIFICATION

Among the most intriguing phenomena in all of world history are the accounts of religious conversion experiences. Some conversions have altered the course of world history: Paul's life-transforming experience on the road to Damascus led to Christianity's expansion throughout the Mediterranean world; Emperor Constantine's deci-

sion to accept Christ as his savior altered the fate of Western civilization; Luther's final discovery of freedom from God's wrath permanently splintered the world's largest religious tradition; King
Ashoka's acceptance of Buddhism preserved the newly developing
faith from possible extinction; Milarepa's conversion has for centuries influenced the religious outlook of Tibetans; and, in more recent
times, the conversion testimonials from individuals such as Anwar
Sadat, Thomas Merton, Eldridge Cleaver, Malcolm X, and innumer-
able sports and entertainment figures have exerted widespread cultural influence. And, of course, these dramatic examples of how
religious conversions have transformed world history should not divert our attention away from the millions of individuals who claim to
have found a new and more fulfilling life through a personal encounter with the divine. In the United States, for example, up to 30 percent of all adults claim to have undergone a dramatic personal
change whereby they proclaimed Jesus Christ as their Savior and, in
so doing, found themselves "born again."[9] Indeed, the very word
"conversion" indicates the complete turning around of an individual's life consequent upon a personal encounter with that which lies
beyond the limits of his or her worldly identity.

Conversions vary greatly among different individuals and different cultural settings. While most are experienced as part of a gradual
development or process, some appear to happen quite suddenly.
Many conversions are accompanied by highly emotional experiences such as crying, shouting, loss of physical control, and "charismatic" activity such as hearing voices, seeing mystical visions, or
speaking in tongues. Others are of a more rational, willful nature and
culminate in a self-conscious intellectual commitment. Some conversions are more or less programmed by a religious institution
through extensive educational experiences (e.g., Sunday school, catechism classes, Bible camp), rituals (e.g., bar mitzvahs, confirma-
tion, adult baptism), or through revival services designed to bring
individuals to the limits of their emotional and intellectual resources, at which time they might open themselves to the whole-
making activity of a Higher Power.

While it is not our present purpose to offer a complete, much less
definitive, psychological interpretation of conversion experiences, it
is important that we appreciate how fully they illustrate the role of

"limit experiences" in directing the course of human development.[10] Whether called the moment of being saved, being regenerated, receiving grace, or being born again, conversions denote a decisive shift in a person's psychological nature. The transformation effected by conversions denotes what William James described as the "process, gradual or sudden, by which a self hitherto divided, and consciously wrong, inferior, and unhappy, becomes unified and consciously right, superior, and happy, *in consequence of* its firmer hold upon religious realities."[11] Religious believers call these transformational processes "stunning acts of God." Religious doctrines concerning salvation and grace teach the futility of relying only on reason and personal will power; we must finally acknowledge our ultimate dependence upon God and surrender our will to him in the faith that he will breathe new life into us and avail us of his gracious spirit. Psychologically oriented persons, on the other hand, tend to view conversions as perfectly lawful stages in personality development through which a person finally escapes the self-centered preoccupations of adolescence and comes to acknowledge the "wider life" which he or she is now entering. According to this point of view, religious communities have simply taken a common stage in personality development and supplied supernatural labels with which an individual might interpret the transition from painful self-consciousness and competing desires to a new sense of unity and the accompanying feelings of relief, assurance, comfort, and so forth.

If we temporarily set aside the question of whether a supernatural agency intervenes in this process of self-unification, we can still appreciate the degree to which conversions originate and function at critical junctures of the life cycle. The conversion process (especially the gradual type) ordinarily begins when the individual comes to the conviction that his or her life is somehow not falling into place. It is, of course, a common human experience to perceive that everyone else's life is heading in the right direction but that our own is off the mark, missing the target. Most of us have at one time or another looked envyingly at almost everyone else, thinking that we and we alone have no prospects of a bright future. Ordinarily we pull out of this gloomy state and find ourselves once again comfortable with ourselves and our lives. However, the second stage toward conversion begins if our sense of meaninglessness or personal inadequacy continues to build. We soon find ourselves engulfed by feelings of loneliness and isolation. We begin to feel "out of touch" with the forces that shape and control life. Furthermore, we see no easy solution to our problems. It strikes us that we are somehow unworthy of a better life, incapable of finding a better future.

At this point we enter a third stage, one of utter despair. Seeing no solutions to our downward spiral we become anxious and despondent. The world closes in and we feel unable to endure the overwhelming sense of self-inadequacy. We now feel judged, condemned, impure, estranged from our intended nature. It is at this point that we lose all confidence in our ability to "will" our way back to feeling whole again solely through our own efforts and emotional resources.

The final stage of the conversion process comes as we simply cease attempting to bring about our own wholeness and instead surrender our will to a Higher Power. This final leap of faith is surprisingly met by a sudden surge of power, confidence, peace, and joy. Consider, for example, the account of Charles Colson. As an aide to former president Richard Nixon, Colson saw his entire personal, family, and political life crumble in the wake of the Watergate scandal. Driven to the point of despair, Colson for the first time learned what it means to be "born again":

> Something began to flow into me—a kind of energy. . . . [While parked alone in a car] with my face cupped in my hands, my head leaning forward against the wheel, I forgot about machismo, about pretenses, about fears of being weak. . . . Then came the strange sensation that water was not only running down my cheeks, but surging through my whole body as well, cleansing and cooling as it went. They weren't tears of sadness nor of joy—but tears of release. I repeated over and over the words "Take me." . . . Something inside me was urging me to surrender. . . . For the first time in my life I was not alone at all.[12]

Former president Jimmy Carter, too, found that he only found his "true self" after first giving over the control of his life to God. After losing a race for the governorship of Georgia, Carter began to think that his whole life was crumbling around him. He came to the realization that "there was just something missing in my life—a sense of peace, a sense of higher purpose."[13] His sister, an evangelical preacher, counseled him to "look beyond yourself for God's purpose.

You've got to be less self-centered in all of your life. . . . You've got to recognize that your mind can't achieve the change you're looking for."[14] Kneeling to pray, he discovered for the first time the deep peace and inner healing that comes from what he calls "a sense of complete dependence on the Holy Spirit."

These, and the thousands of other such accounts of the turning around of one's life through the gracious activity of a Higher Power, stand as powerful testimony of the limit character of some of the most profound experiences through which humans achieve integration and wholeness. On strictly psychological grounds, of course, the fact that individuals experience this healing as coming from beyond themselves is by no means proof that a spiritual presence or energy is at work. From the psychological perspective, the curative forces acting at these moments can be considered to be simply aspects of one's own personality that are at long last being released and acknowledged. Because so much of our personality is unconscious, it can be argued that the mind's own curative activities are mistakenly perceived as "beyond" our ordinary waking self. Yet it should be pointed out that recognizing the role unconscious psychological processes undoubtedly do play in producing conversions does not necessarily disprove the religious belief that a supernatural agency such as God is ultimately responsible for these dramatic transformations in personality. After all, these psychological processes might well be the very mechanisms through which an extrapsychological agency exerts its influence within the structure of human personality. As James so aptly observed, "Just as our primary wide-awake consciousness throws open our senses to the touch of things material, so it is logically conceivable that *if there be* higher spiritual agencies that can directly touch us, the psychological condition of this doing so *might be* our possession of a subconscious region which alone should yield access to them."[15] In other words, the fact that natural laws and causes can be used to help explain how or why individuals come to believe that they have experienced a supernatural reality does not necessarily explain that reality away—quite the contrary. It simply implies that the "natural" structures of personality are in some fundamental way susceptible of influences from a spiritual agency that lies beyond them. We might best leave this controversial topic by concluding that, in either case, religious conversions are in fact among the most dramatic of all psychological processes in terms of their impact upon the subsequent course and direction of the life cycle.

MYSTICISM AND THE STRENUOUS LIFE

In the previous chapter we noted the extent to which happiness in the latter half of the life cycle depends upon our ability to attain new and less egoistic perspectives upon our lives. The search for meaning, the attainment of a developed moral sense, and the quest for vision and wisdom in the face of death all require a gradual transformation of our cognitive grasp of reality. In each case adaptation to life's deepest challenges and mysteries were seen to hinge upon our ability to take a universal or cosmic perspective. And, in each case, these developmental stages evoked modes of thought that were not so much rational as mystical insofar as they entailed the attempt to view life from "beyond" its physical appearances.

Such transformations in our modes of apprehending reality are not, however, always occasioned by developmental challenges. The records of human history are replete with accounts of individuals who have quite suddenly and unexpectedly found themselves engaged in the mystical apprehension of a More. What characterizes an experience as mystical is the breakdown of the ordinary waking state of consciousness dominated by information supplied by the physical senses. In the normal waking state, reality is apprehended in terms of the psychological structures that select, limit, organize, and interpret perceptual stimuli. A mystical state is one in which these psychological structures are temporarily dismantled, coupled with the activation of perceptual capacities responsive to ranges of stimuli ordinarily ignored or blocked from awareness.[16] Because mystical states have a cognitive structure quite different from that of the normal waking state, they have an ineffable quality about them and cannot be literally described or communicated to others with words drawn from our conventional vocabularies. Yet, even though mystical experiences are ineffable, they nonetheless leave long-lasting impressions upon those individuals who have had them. They carry with them types of insights, illuminations, and revelations to which the rational intellect is blind. And, thus, though they remain unarticulated, mystical states of mind are considered by those who have them to bear a particular kind of experiential knowledge. There is, it would seem, a kind of continuum along which mystical experiences range. A relatively "light" mystical state often arises while hearing a favorite poem or engaging in types of athletic activity that cause us to let go of our ordinary sense of self-consciousness. Alcoholic intoxication, hypnotic reverie, dreamy fantasy, and drug-induced modes of perception all represent successive stages along the path toward mystical consciousness. The fullest expression, however, is to be found in the saint or religious virtuoso. The Hindu yogin's descriptions of the state of samadhi, the Zen practitioner's account of satori, and the Christian ascetic's experience of the mystical body of Christ are all examples of the attainment of a state of consciousness quite distinct from that of the ordinary waking condition. Labeling this mystical mode of perception "cosmic consciousness," R. M. Bucke described it in this way:

> The prime characteristic of cosmic consciousness is a consciousness of the cosmos, that is, of the life and order of the universe. Along with the consciousness of the cosmos there occurs an intellectual enlightenment which alone would place the individual on a new plane of existence— would make him almost a member of a new species. To this is added a state of moral exaltation, an indescribable feeling of elevation, elation, and joyousness, and a quickening of the moral sense.[17]

As Bucke's description indicates, mystical consciousness is not so much consciousness of a specific object in the universe as it is the overpowering sensation of encountering that "life and order" by which there is a universe at all. It is an awareness not of a particular being, but of the spiritual power expressing itself in all of being. This apprehension that the whole of our physical universe is animated by a spiritual More invariably exerts long-lasting influences upon our conceptions of ourselves and the world we live in. Bucke described his own mystical experience as affording him the insight

> that the universe is not composed of dead matter, but is, on the contrary, a living Presence; I became conscious in myself of eternal life. It was not a conviction that I would have eternal life, but a consciousness that I possessed eternal life then; I saw that all men are immortal; that the cosmic order is such that without any peradventure all things work together for the good of each and all.[18]

James called the type of character produced by this shift in consciousness "saintliness." Examining the lives of saintly persons from all religious traditions, he observed that there is a lawful pattern to the psychological transformation wrought by mystical apprehensions of the divine: (1) a feeling of being in a wider life than that apprehended through the rational ego accompanied by a deep conviction of the existence of an Ideal Power; (2) a sense of the friendly continuity of this ideal power with our own life, and a willing self-surrender to its control; (3) an immense elation and freedom, as the outlines of the confining selfhood melt down; and, finally, (4) a shifting of the emotional center toward loving affections, strength of soul, charity, purity, and willingness to sacrifice personal comfort in the service of a higher good.[19]

The fruits born of mystical experience are, according to James, the clearest examples of "the genuinely strenuous life." The transcendence of egoistic concerns and the acquired capacity to identify with the whole of living creation dissipate any tendency toward the easy-going mood. The mystical apprehension of a More or Ideal Power makes service and self-sacrifice a privilege rather than a burden. For this reason, "the highest flights of charity, devotion, trust, patience, bravery to which the wings of human nature have spread themselves have been flown for religious ideals."[20] The saintly character is one in which indifference has given way to compassion, passivity to active service, and defensiveness to aggressive concern for others. As we noted in the last chapter when reviewing Lawrence Kohlberg's studies of moral development, the mid- or late-life transition to a "cosmic moral perspective" such as would constitute the very pinnacle of moral development requires precisely this mystical "union of the mind with the whole of nature." And thus even though many saintly individuals are ill-adapted to their social and economic surroundings owing to their overly gentle and peaceful dispositions, they are nonetheless leavens of a better and higher world.

We might in conclusion consider what James thought to be the three major implications that mystical experiences have for our interpretation of the nature and meaning of human existence.[21] First, we must acknowledge that mystical states usually are, and have the right to be, absolutely authoritative over the individuals who experience them. Regardless of anyone's objections to mysticism's lack of rational content, it is nonetheless an experience that carries its own internal validation as a legitimate form of knowledge. Second, however, the experiential character of the "knowledge" that comes from mystical states is such that it carries no intellectual authority that must be acknowledged uncritically by others. Any truth-claim offered by those who have undergone a mystical experience is subject to the same rational and empirical standards of knowledge as any other belief or opinion. The attempt to translate the content of a mystical experience from the "private" to the "public" realm severs its truth from the context in which it was received and obliges it to be judged by its ability to integrate with the contours of common human experience. Third, and finally, mystical experiences break down the authority of the nonmystical or rationalistic consciousness based on sensory experience alone. Mystical experiences show the normal waking state of consciousness to be but one kind of consciousness; they suggest that although the normal waking state is well suited to the task of adapting us to the physical environment, it is for that very reason poorly suited to the perception of other configurations of reality. As James discerned,

> Our normal waking consciousness, rational consciousness as we call it, is but one special type of consciousness, whilst all about it, parted from it by the filmiest of screens, there lie potential forms of consciousness entirely different. . . . It must always remain an open question whether mystical states may not possibly be superior points of view, windows through which the mind looks out upon a more extensive and inclusive world.[22]

Consciousness is, after all, our sole guide to reality. The farther reaches of human consciousness would thus seem to hold important hints, which should be taken into account in any attempt to understand the universe in its totality.

RELIGION, TRANSFORMATION, AND THE SELF

Limit experiences of the sort we have been considering—peak experiences, conversions, and mysticism—are not readily incorporated into the mainstream of modern academic psychology. The attempt to be as "scientific" as possible has made it difficult for modern psychology to study, or even acknowledge, experiences that cannot be objectively observed, measured, and quantitatively examined. In fact, much of academic psychology goes under the label "behavioral science" to indicate clearly its belief that only observable behaviors can be considered the proper subject matter of science. It should be remembered that psychology emerged as an independent academic discipline at the turn of this century precisely by defining itself over and against both philosophy and theology. It was argued that the nonscientific character of philosophical and religious perspectives on human nature made it necessary to create a "psychology without a soul."

The decision to model psychology along the lines of the natural sciences simultaneously committed psychology to a number of philosophical assumptions that have prevented it from judging humanity's recurrent experiences of a More beyond the limits of our ordinary sensory experience to have any validity or importance.[23] For example, the model of human nature underlying orthodox Western psychology assumes that humans are lawfully determined by the combined influence of their genetic inheritance and social environment. The human is assumed to be a physical organism and nothing more. It follows that the only knowledge of which humans are capable is that which is based upon information presented to the brain through the physical senses. The conscious, rational mind is the pinnacle of humanity's evolutionary development and is thus the only reliable vehicle through which to know reality; all other states of consciousness, because they are deviations from the normal waking state, produce distorted and unreliable forms of experience. Each of us is a separate individual, isolated from all others by virtue of being "locked" within our separate bodies and nervous systems; there is, therefore, no real sense in which humans could be said to be united with one another. Science knows of no "higher reason" for life and it follows that there is no sense in discussing the purpose or meaning of life other than what we arbitrarily decide to make through our own efforts. And, finally, death is the end of human life; discussion of survival after death is from the scientific point of view meaningless.

The basic paradigm or theoretical model underlying most of contemporary psychology is thus linked part and parcel with a bias toward the normal waking state of consciousness. A scientific paradigm, like a state of consciousness, is a complex set of interpretations which distinguish between relevant and irrelevant aspects of experience. Paradigms, like states of consciousness, develop through experience and tend to become implicit "definers" of reality rather than explicit attempts to organize experience into helpful patterns. And paradigms, like states of consciousness, operate by excluding and filtering out information and thus not only give credence to concepts that adhere to its limitations but also undermine concepts based upon information not included within their carefully defined limits.

It is important to note that modern psychology's commitment to the cognitive activities associated with the normal waking state biases it toward a positivistic model of human experience. It consequently pictures the self in terms commensurate with sensory experience. That is, the self is interpreted as an entity which can be defined in terms of the causal influences that originate in the physical organism and the social environment. It is possible to speak of what we have been referring to as "final cause" explanations of the self insofar, and only insofar, as psychological structures internal to the organism such as sustained attention, will, personality type, attitude, and so forth, can be shown to exert observable differences in behavior.

The limit experiences we have been considering differ from the ordinary waking state of consciousness in that they register a nonsensory awareness of an "ultimate" context or environment from which humanity derives its existence and meaning. And, too, they disclose to awareness a fundamental sense in which our well-being ultimately depends upon our relationship to, or connection with, this nonsensory reality. To this extent limit experiences are necessarily convictional in nature; they impress upon us an awareness or consciousness of an ultimate reality which exists over and beyond the limits of the finite, rational ego. And, insofar as they suggest that there are psychological states or modes of knowing equal or even superior to the normal waking state in terms of producing human satisfaction, they simultaneously suggest that psychology has been premature in excluding "ultimate" cause explanations from its theoretical framework.

There is, of course, the question of the validity of limit experiences. One way of putting this question is to ask how they might fit

into an empirically based model of human nature. The term philosophical anthropology refers to the attempt to conceptualize human
existence in ways that are sufficiently generalized to account for the
principal structures and processes through which human nature develops. Insofar as limit experiences suggest the existence of nonsensory or metaphysical dimensions of human development, they need
to be assessed for their compatibility with other known psychological foundations of a comprehensive model of human nature. While
an exhaustive analysis of this issue is beyond the scope of this book,
two independent lines of inquiry can be briefly sketched. First, we
might consider the function of limit experiences in terms of promoting personal integration. It can be argued, on empirical grounds
alone, that limit experiences are the primary means whereby humans acquire the very ontological convictions that psychological
theory demonstrates are the necessary conditions of healthy development. That is, they disclose to human awareness vivid insights
concerning such developmental themes as trust/hope, integrity/wis-
dom, meaning, moral commitment, and so forth. They are for this
reason alone indispensable elements of a fully empirical philosophical anthropology. Second, it would appear that limit experiences
elicit transformations that not only conform to, but are perhaps even
paradigmatic of, the developmental transitions that mark human becoming as instigated by material, environmental, and attitudinal
factors. In this way they both articulate well with the findings of scientific psychology and also shed additional light concerning the ultimate ontological laws and principles that make the life process
possible.

Religion, it can be argued, represents the most complete form of
personal integration. Whereas for Freud psychological integration
had to do with the ego's capacity to regulate instinctual gratification
in a prudent fashion, subsequent psychoanalytic theorists have sub-
ordinated the importance of instinctual dynamics to the individual's
mode of relating to others in the context of personal relationships.
"Object relations" theorists such as Melanie Klein, W. R. Fairbairn,
and D. W. Winnicott have demonstrated that personal development
is in large part a function of growth in the medium of personal relationships. The achievement of integration during this ongoing process is dependent upon forms of personal relating that maximize one's

sense of being a prized and yet autonomous person. As the psychoanalytic theorist H. Guntrip has observed, "For good or ill, the universe has begotten us with an absolute need to be able to relate in fully personal terms to an environment that we feel relates beneficially to us."[24] In other words, human beings have an absolute need for a *personal* environment that values us as persons, if we are to be able to become and survive as *persons*. Whatever else religious experience is, it is a representation of relationship. Religious experience imparts the conviction that the environing universe constitutes a world in which *persons* can feel at home with a sense of belonging. Peak experiences, conversions, and mysticism all represent transformational states of consciousness in that they present the world to us not as an assembly of extrinsic objects which are related to each other through their various utilitarian functions, but rather as complementary expressions of one intrinsically meaningful spiritual presence. This insight led James to conclude that, at a single stroke, religious experience "changes the dead blank *it* of the world into a living *thou*, with whom the whole man may have dealings."[25]

It is, in fact, quite possible to argue that the fullest personal integration and maturity necessarily builds upon a distinctively religious way of experiencing the world. Psychoanalytic object relations theory makes clear that what we mean by the idea of self or personhood is the sense of individuality which emerges early in life through our relationships with objects and persons in our environment. The "crisis" of selfhood emerges as we first discover our separateness from the nurturing parent and seek to maintain a sense of being a prized, warm self through union with a valued "other" while yet simultaneously preserving independence and autonomy. Meeting this twofold need upon which personhood depends requires a nonrational engagement with life such that the ontic safety first felt in relationship to the parent is also experienced in the ever-expanding environment. In chapter 1 we noted the developmental need for a "transitional object" (often fulfilled in childhood by a doll, teddy bear, or imaginary friend) which creates the trust or safety needed to extend one's personhood outward into the world. Religious experience imparts convictional knowledge of the existence of an ultimate presence or power which imbues the environment with this transitional quality.

Religion therefore relates us to a world which is itself the expression of an ultimately valuable "other." And, as James observed, for this reason there is "not an energy of our active nature to which it does not authoritatively appeal, not an emotion of which it does not normally and naturally release the springs."[26]

The second reason for assuming the "validity" of limit or religious experiences for a sound philosophical anthropology is the manner in which they disclose the logical structure of the entire developmental process.[27] Throughout the course of life, development consists of the ongoing process whereby emerging organic potentials are brought into an equilibrium with environmental demands. New potentials or new demands disrupt an earlier equilibrium and thereby require the individual to acquire adaptive or relational abilities for extending its successful transactions with the environment. Erikson's description of the sequence whereby we acquire the developmental strengths of autonomy, initiative, industry, identity, intimacy, and generativity capitulates the major stages through which the self-sufficiency of an earlier stage is disrupted and demands a more differentiated mode of engaging the world. Yet the alpha and the omega of this process, the acquisition of basic trust and a felt-sense of integrity, differ from the other six in a fundamental sense. Each requires not the assimilation of knowledge and skills that can be communicated through the socialization process, but rather an experiential conviction of the trustworthiness and meaningfulness of what is "other" than the finite, rational self.

Religious experience recapitulates the basic developmental sequence whereby a former equilibrium is disrupted, followed by the acquisition of adaptive skills which establish new modes for participation in an ever-widening environment. The limit character of religious experience disrupts the cognitive structures of the normal waking state. By imparting a convictional knowledge of an Ultimate Other from which wholeness is received rather than created, religious experience throws sensory-based strategies for adapting to life out of balance. Yet, simultaneously, religious experience affords a new and vital sense of relatedness to, or even participation in, a wholeness-bestowing reality that lies beyond the boundaries of the self. In this way the limit character of religious experiences makes possible the continuation of the developmental process whereby new

orders of life succeed upon one another even in the face of the dissolution of the finite self. Thus when a psychologist such as Carl Jung
refers to the developmental process as the gradual manifestation of
the Self that transcends the finite ego or a theologian such as Paul refers to the ego's ultimate transformation through an experience of relationship with Christ, they are stating their conviction that the ego
is inherently incapable of centering the personality throughout its
course from birth to death. In each case they are asking us to broaden
our sense of the world to include the metaphysical "other" upon
which life is not just provisionally, but ultimately, dependent. Put
this way, the developmental process is itself the activity whereby this
Other progressively creates meaning in the world. Divine creativity,
it would seem, is ongoing and each of our own life cycles has almost
limitless potential for participating in, and perhaps even contributing to, this aspect of the divine plan for humanity. Religious experiences disrupt the normal waking state's organization of the causal
forces governing our existence and thereby help to disclose our participation in this process. And, for this reason, they afford the vital
link in any attempt to ask just what ontological or metaphysical purpose the life cycle and its developmental structures might serve.

SIX

RELIGION AND THE ART
OF LIFE CYCLE
MAINTENANCE

Up to this point we have restricted our discussion of religion to the limit dimension of human experience. Defining religion in terms of commonly occurring human experiences has enabled us to generate an empirical framework for understanding the origin and function of religion within the total context of the life cycle. The focus of our study, however, has been exclusively on the individual and the ways in which spiritual values and experiences of transcendence emerge throughout the course of the life cycle. This final chapter will consider religion as a social or cultural force independent of the individual. After all, religion (whether institutionalized in formal organizations or existing as an informal aspect of a culture's total way of life) stands alongside the family, schools, and government as one of the social institutions most likely to influence human development and shape the way we pursue happiness and fulfillment. And it is possible at this point in our study to use developmental concepts to assess the nature and meaning of such religious activities as worship, prayer, ritual, and the ministry.

Religion differs from other cultural institutions in that it divides life into two more or less separate dimensions: the secular and the sacred. The secular aspects of life consist of all those activities that can be perceived and analyzed from the perspective of the rational mind.

From the religious point of view, the economic, social, and political aspects of life are all secular in that they are ordinarily pursued without reference to anything beyond the limits of the finite, physical world. The sacred, meanwhile, confronts humans as that which lies beyond the limits of ordinary human experience. It is perceived as the final or ultimate causal power of existence, producing ecstasy in those who momentarily experience it. The sacred has a transformative power. Experiencing the sacred gives rise to qualitatively distinct sensations of holiness, purity, and power. Most persons report that finding inner harmony with the sacred promotes physical, mental, and emotional healing and thus revitalizes them for strenuous participation in growth-promoting activities.

What distinguishes religion from philosophy, psychology, or sociology as a guide toward human betterment is that it views the sacred as the principal sphere to which humans ought to adapt themselves. That is, religion insists that our highest possibilities come only by establishing a harmonious relationship with a sacred power existing beyond the limits of the finite personality. The various world religions represent the diverse ways in which humans have institutionalized both their belief in the sacred and their understanding of those activities which can best bring us into increased harmony or participation in its transformative powers. Religions witness to their belief in the sacred by performing a twofold cultural function: (1) they make the ecstasy found in personal contact with the sacred available to individuals on a regular and consistent basis; and (2) they seek to bring this felt-sense of the sacred to bear upon the developmental needs not only of individuals but also of the larger community. Among the principal ways through which religions accomplish these tasks are rituals, prayer, meditation, and traditions of ministry, guidance, and counseling.

WORSHIP AS RITUALIZED
LIMIT EXPERIENCES

The life of any religious tradition is to be found in its forms of worship and ritual. Worship is the act of bringing one's total existence into harmony with the ultimate powers and patterns operative in the universe. It involves shifting the focus of one's personal identity away from preoccupation with everyday concerns and opening one-self to a holy reality at the far limits of human rationality. We might say that in the act of worship our awareness shifts away from the challenges of worldly becoming to an awe-inspiring recognition of the miracle of Being. Worship involves the sense of approaching and becoming receptive to a spiritual influence entering our lives from beyond or above. For this reason it infuses personal life with a new zest and enthusiasm. As Rufus Jones describes in his *The World Within,* worship is a process of self-renewal that should be regarded as a special and necessary activity whereby individuals find a firsthand knowledge of the availability of God's spiritual presence.

> By worship I mean the act of rising to a personal, experiential consciousness of the real presence of God which floods the soul with joy and bathes the whole inward spirit with refreshing streams of life. Never to have felt that, never to have opened life to these incoming divine tides, never to have experienced the joy of personal fellowship with God, is surely to have missed the richest privilege and the highest beatitude of religion.[1]

The attitudes associated with worship can and do appear spontaneously within individuals (such as Maslow described in his studies of peak experiences) without any need for institutionalized religion. However, nearly every human society has developed ritualized forms of worship through which its members can be guided periodically to such experiences of contact with the sacred. Although we often use the word "ritual" to refer to any set of repeated behaviors (e.g., family rituals such as annual Christmas tree decorating, daily exercise programs, etc.), the word is being used here solely in its religious connotations as a structured form of worship. Rituals provide a framework within which we can suspend secular existence and create awareness of the presence of the sacred. We might say that by participating in rituals we step out of our ordinary identities and temporarily participate in a higher, sacred order of life.

The noted anthropologist Victor Turner views rituals in terms of their function within the lives of individuals and communities. There are, he suggests, two somewhat opposing ways in which humans relate to one another.[2] The first of these he calls "structure." By structure Turner means the laws, rules, and principles necessary for regulating social existence. Because humans will always compete for limited economic resources, there is a need for social structures capable of regulating our relationships in ways that minimize conflict. Social structures impose certain responsibilities, ethical duties, and behavioral codes upon us for the purpose of communal stability. Life in "structure," however, has a tendency to drain us of our vitality, spontaneity, and uncoerced spirit of friendship and love. Because social structures channel our relationships with others into role-bound patterns of interaction, they foster a certain impersonality in communal life. In this sense "structure" tends to deplete us of our most human qualities and over time leads to resentments, friction, and dispiritedness.

The second major mode of human existence is that of "communitas." Communitas consists of that bond of friendship and love without which there could be no society. It is the spirit of human-kindness that fosters a sense of unity and commonality among individuals. Turner notes that communitas is felt as a distinct, separate mode of consciousness. It breaks into human lives in those moments when we have temporarily suspended our structured habits of thought and action. From the religious point of view communitas represents the activity of a sacred or holy presence and, in fact, Turner notes that almost everywhere humans attribute communitas to the influx of a divine spirit into the human realm. Communitas reinvigorates lives that have been drained of vitality by the rigidities of social structure. It transforms the "I-It" character of role-structured relationships into "I-Thou" encounters characterized by selfless love. And, finally, communitas infects individual life with a sense of boundless, mystical power capable of stimulating us to new levels of growth and creativity.

What rituals do, according to Turner, is release individuals temporarily from life in structure and provide them with a felt-sense of communitas. As the ritual concludes individuals feel refreshed, reinvigorated, and ready to resume their normal social roles and responsibilities with a renewed sense of the precious quality of interpersonal relationships. Turner observes that the "ritual process" consists of three distinct phases which he calls those of separation, margin, and reaggregation. The separation phase of a ritual signifies a person's departure from "things as usual." For example, when individuals stand up and walk to a church altar they approach holy space, sacred symbols, and a person ordained in God's ministry; they have temporarily separated themselves from secular life. Entrance into a sacred building, the wearing of special clothing, the presence of special music, or the use of a special language, all help symbolize a person's separation from socially structured reality. The second stage of the ritual process is the experience of being beyond the limits of life in structure and of being immersed in the spirit of communitas. The marginal phase exists outside of human space and time; it invokes the feelings of infinity and eternity. The purpose of this phase of a religious ritual is in some way to bring the participant into harmony or communion with the sacred. Various religious traditions have developed their own unique symbols and rites for accomplishing this task but they share in common the goal of inducing a mystical state of consciousness in which individuals might come to feel their lives to be grounded in a sacred presence common to all of humanity. The third and final stage of the ritual process is that of reincorporating an individual into his or her accustomed social roles. Having taken a person "beyond" his or her ordinary identity, the ritual must in some way conclude by signifying the resumption of duties and responsibilities of life in structure. This reaggregation of social roles and duties is, however, facilitated by the life-spirit acquired or renewed during the state of existing in the margin between the finite and infinite realms. The importance of this stage is that it reminds us that humans cannot live permanently in the sacred. The purpose of rituals is to introduce the sacred into our day-to-day lives, ennoble them, and reveal their ultimate significance and direction. Rituals must, however, finally reaffirm the spiritual significance of the realm of human becoming and teach us to view our life in structure as potentially contributing to the sacred dimensions of existence.

The power of rituals lies in their ability to induct individuals into a sacred reality that stands over against the structures of secular existence. Leaving behind the sense of limitation, ambiguity, and transitoriness of everyday life, persons come into direct contact with the expansive qualities of divine spirit. The invocation or opening words of a worship service signals one's separation from mundane reality and stimulates expectations of an imminent encounter with the divine. During the service one is in the marginal state of being beyond the limits of ordinary social roles and identities. The priest, rabbi, or minister invokes the spirit of communitas through sacred words and gestures. As individuals progressively let go of their ordinary rational controls (fostered by music, responsive readings, and the very act of having entered the "sacred space" of the church or synagogue) they feel themselves becoming open or receptive to a purifying spiritual presence. The service reinforces the belief that our very being can be transformed and uplifted by bringing it into harmony with God's spirit and reminds us that in God's eyes all humans are one. As the worship service closes a benediction is offered signaling the reaggregation of our secular lives and responsibilities and exhorting us to resume them with an intensified commitment to love, peace, and charity.

There are, of course, many types of religious rituals other than those of worship and sacrament. For example, some serve primarily instructional or commemorative functions such as Christian Christmas pageants or the Jewish Seder dinner. A high percentage of the rituals performed in every religious tradition are intended to guide and structure important transitional stages in the life cycle. Usually referred to as rites of passage, these rituals employ the phases of separation, margin, and reaggregation to assist individuals through the major critical stages of human development. Hindus, for example, recognize forty such changes in a person's status or social role, ranging from the moment of conception to physical death. In Christianity, five of the seven traditional sacraments involve sacralizing major transitions in the life cycle. Judaism and Islam likewise commemorate such events as marriage, ordination, or death with appropriate rites of passage. In each case the individual is in some way removed or separated from his or her former role and temporarily set apart for the purpose of instruction or sacramental purification. Having been fortified by the wisdom and spiritual blessing of the religious community, the individual is now prepared to assume a new role or status in the society. Baptisms, confirmations, bar mitzvahs, marriage ceremonies, ordinations to holy ministry, and funeral ceremonies are all rites of passage whereby religious congregations assure individuals of successful adaptations to new roles or social responsibilities (or, in the case of death, a harmonious transition beyond the life cycle).[3]

RITUALS AND "CREATIVE FORMALIZATION"
THROUGHOUT THE LIFE CYCLE

One of Erik Erikson's most important contributions to developmental psychology has been his explicit recognition of the role ritual plays in eliciting psychological growth. Before Erikson, Freud had drawn attention to the ways rituals—particularly religious rituals—closely resemble the behaviors of neurotic obsession. Freud argued that in each case there is a compulsion to repeat unresolved conflicts which are ultimately rooted in our efforts to repress unconscious urges and desires.[4] Freud concluded that rituals, as with other compulsive behaviors, are symptoms of psychological maladjustment and that individuals who can gain rational insight into their conflicts will no longer need to engage in ritual activity. Erikson, however, has noted a fundamental difference between religious rituals and the ritual-like behavior of neurotic persons.[5] Whereas neurotic rituals are carried out in self-imposed solitude, religious rituals draw persons out into communal activity and shared meaning. For this reason Erikson contends that religious rituals perform very different psychological functions from those Freud had assumed and, in fact, can be seen to be paradigmatic instances of the ways in which cultures give rise to ritualized customs designed to integrate their young into a world of meaningful actions and symbolic meanings.

For Erikson, then, ritualization consists of what he calls the "creative formalization" whereby a culture provides growth-inducing experiences for its members. Central to this theory of ritual is the idea that ritualization takes on new forms and new meanings as individuals progress through the life cycle. Erikson detects eight separate elements in ritualization—each of which roughly corresponds to one of the eight stages in his model of the life cycle. The formalized activities whereby communities seek to elicit meaningful growth in their members must, according to Erikson, have elements of the numinous (corresponding to the need for basic trust), the judicious (autonomy and freedom from shame or doubt), the dramatic (initiative), the formal (industry), the ideological (identity), the affiliative (generativity), and the integral (integrity). It should be pointed out, however, that the eight major virtues Erikson discerns as necessary adaptive strengths remain vital themes of psychological health throughout our lives. And thus although the various elements of ritualization might be most salient to us at particular stages of development, they would nonetheless retain their strength-bestowing power throughout the course of our lives.

We might, for example, examine how the first element Erikson believes to be indispensable to effective rituals—the numinous—relates to the patterns of human becoming. Beginning with infancy, individuals again and again encounter the disorienting experience of separation or abandonment. Mothers soon learn to greet their infants in highly ritualized ways that communicate their presence, availability, and comforting recognition. Erikson contends that these early rituals of mutual recognition provide the developmental foundations for the numinous experience in which the individual looks "for somebody to look up to, somebody who will, in the very act of returning his glance, lift him up."[6] The discovery of face-to-face recognition is fraught with awe, comfort, peace, and surrender to a higher power. Nearly all periodic observances build upon this dynamic of recognition and engage this same emotional sense of devotion and assurance. As Donald Capps has observed in his creative application of Erikson's work for a theory of pastoral care, "The goal of true ritualization in this stage is not the total elimination of the sense of separation and abandonment but regular and consistent assurance that our separateness has been transcended (through face-to-face recognition and being lifted up) and our distinctiveness confirmed (through being called by name)."[7] It should be fairly evident that nearly every major worship activity (baptism, the Seder dinner, communion, funeral) has a strong element of the numinous. And, in this way, rituals respond to our psychological need for recognition and assurance by providing continuous experiences of being enveloped by God's confirming presence.

In a similar fashion, each of the other seven elements of ritualization correspond to the major disruptions encountered over the course of the life cycle. Donald Capps has reviewed Erikson's distinctive understanding of the eight elements of "creative formalization" and emphasized the way in which rabbis, ministers, or priests serve as "ritual coordinators" by bringing the resources of religion to bear upon critical junctures of the developmental process. Capps points out that church communities provide ritual resolutions to developmental needs in many more ways than through their weekly worship services, baptisms, weddings, funerals, and so on. Congregations also formalize their care for the human life cycle through coffee hours, pastoral counseling, study groups, informal social gatherings, and educational programs. Through all of these means religious communities ritualize their conviction that such vital themes as identity, generativity, and wisdom are actualized through continuous encounter with the sacred.

PSYCHOLOGICAL CONSIDERATIONS
OF PRAYER

Prayer is undoubtedly the most spontaneous expression of religion. It is also the most difficult to assess from the perspective of individual development across the life cycle. Studies indicate that more than 85 percent of us pray at least once in a while.[8] Yet our reasons for praying vary so greatly as to complicate efforts to examine its impact upon emotional or psychological health. For example, one study showed that nearly a third of us pray because we believe that God listens to and answers our prayers.[9] An additional fifty percent of us, although a little less confident that prayer moves God to act in our behalf, say that we pray because it makes us feel better and helps us through times of stress and crisis. Smaller percentages of us say that we pray because it reminds us of our moral obligations and because we think that it is an activity that good persons are expected to do.

When examining persons' motivations to pray, psychologist Walter Houston Clark concluded that the vast majority of prayers have little or nothing to do with religious worship. Few prayers represent the desire to harmonize our lives with that which is Beyond the limits of the physical universe.[10] Instead, most prayers seem to represent the confusion of magical ideas with religion. Rather than indicating a genuine encounter with the limit dimension of human experience, they express wishful thinking that our every desire will be magically fulfilled if we but recite the right words with enough sincerity. Freud observed the magical or superstitious aspects of prayer in so many individuals that he came to the conclusion that religion was in fact nothing more than a psychologically immature approach to the harsh realities of life. Prayer, Freud thought, reveals the perpetuation of childlike attitudes into adult life. Just as children beg, plead, and make promises to their parents in order to get their own way, so do many adults attempt to beg, plead with, and make promises to their "Heavenly Father" in order to have their needs magically taken care of for them. Small wonder that Freud believed that prayer, as with childhood begging, is an irrational form of thinking that should be abandoned in favor of rational, problem-solving approaches to life.

No doubt there is a great deal of validity to these criticisms concerning the psychologically immature character of prayer. It might be helpful, however, to differentiate among several different types of prayer. Because each type of prayer has its own psychological characteristics, we should evaluate them accordingly. We can, for example, divide prayers into five more or less distinct categories: prayers of petition, prayers of intercession, prayers of confession and repentance, prayers of praise and thanksgiving, and prayers of communion. Prayers of petition entail requesting God to help us acquire some desired object, status, or condition. They are for this reason the most egocentric of all prayers and may possibly have little or nothing genuinely religious about them. Rather than seeking to expand the self toward its limit dimensions, prayers of petition seek to coerce an external force into magically altering the natural order of things for our own worldly purposes. Prayers of intercession are a variation of petitionary prayers in that they seek no help for oneself but rather for someone else. A common example of an intercessory prayer is when we pray for God to help a loved one recover from a serious illness. Such a prayer, while helping to vent our feelings of helplessness in times of emergency, is yet difficult to defend against charges of being superstitious and based upon magical thinking. Prayers of confession and repentance permit a catharsis of pent-up feelings of guilt, inferiority, and shame. By confessing our shortcomings to God and pledging to reform we feel lightened of a burden and free to start anew in our efforts to live a righteous life. It is not always clear, however, whether the motivation is in any way distinctively religious or simply a means of resolving tensions arising from our superego or conscience.

Prayers of praise and thanksgiving are more likely to involve transcendence of self-centered preoccupations. This is especially the case when the praise and thanksgiving are offered not for specific external "blessings" but rather as spontaneous responses to the perception of life's intrinsic creativity and design. In such moments awareness shifts away from the self and its immediate needs toward the ultimate horizons of human dependence. Prayers of communion express the desire to harmonize with the sacred even more directly. The quest for communion represents the attempt to open one's life to the More of our psychological experience and become receptive to its higher, regenerative powers. Prayers of communion, as with those of praise and thanksgiving, potentially can transform a secondhand religious faith into a living awareness of the availability of a wider spiritual environment from which we might derive our highest happiness and fulfillment. Prayer can occasion a limit experience of the positive or expansive kind in which we find ourselves immediately and directly confronted with a More existing beyond our ordinary sensory experience. For this reason prayers of communion may well be the definitive expression of the distinctively religious approach to life. As the late Protestant theologian Nels Ferre maintained,

> Prayer is the main highway to making religion real. Unless we meet God in prayer, we never meet Him, for prayer is meeting God. Unless we meet Him, He can never become real to us. A person can be fully real to us only as we get to know him personally. . . . To be sure, God is always and everywhere present as the one who creates, sustains, and controls the world. But as such He is not personally present. We can meet God personally only in communion with Him and such communion is prayer.[11]

Compounding the difficulty of considering prayer psychologically is that most prayers presuppose a religious belief system outside the conceptual scope of scientific psychology. The existence or nonexistence of a Supreme Being to which the vast majority of prayers are addressed is not capable of being ascertained on psychological grounds. The fact that humans claim to experience such a Being does not alone establish its reality. We must, therefore, restrict our assessment of prayer to its functions within the structures of personality. Yet, even on psychological grounds, it is possible to ascertain at least three ways in which prayer promotes healthy development across the life span. First, prayer is a privatized form of ritual that facilitates our temporary separation from the stresses and strains of everyday life. Prayer establishes a safe, secure emotional environment in which we might let down our defenses and learn to see ourselves in more realistic ways. Under these conditions of existing at the margins of our normal identity, we can privately release our fears, worries, and feelings of inadequacy. A catharsis of this sort alone is therapeutic and helps marshal recuperative energies. Second, prayers help us to focus upon and clarify our desires, intentions, and aspirations. The period of quiet, introspective analysis fosters our ability to forgo immediate, but shortsighted, impulses and instead commit ourselves to courses of action that will insure long-term benefits both to ourselves and to others. Third, prayer is in many respects an extension of the normal psychological process of identification. Throughout the course of personality development we form identifications with parents, siblings, peers, sports or entertainment idols, and so forth, and incorporate their attributes into our own personality structures. Prayer widens this field of identification to include God. In prayer we find ourselves identified with the very source of goodness and creativity. For this reason prayer fosters both self-acceptance and the attainment of a healthy self-concept. Not only can prayer promote a heightened sense of self-worth, but it can also help us identify with God's will or plan for the universe. In this way prayer assists us in gradually moving toward a universal, rather than self-centered, moral perspective. And, by opening up our world to include that which lies Beyond the limits of our ordinary psychological environment, prayer can make it possible for us to achieve the kind of wisdom that is alone capable of calmly affirming the life cycle in its entirety, including the losses endured through aging and death.

MEDITATION AND SELF-RENEWAL

The term meditation is often used as a synonym for prayers of communion. In each case the individual seeks not to petition God for specific favors, but to discover our place in the divine plan. Meditation intends to establish not a monologue, but a dialogue; not an intensified moment of asking, but serenity through which to listen and

receive. Both represent the individual's intention to approach the sacred not for the purpose of producing magical alterations in the outer
world, but to receive a new vision and new strength that will enable
us to be our own agents of change and betterment.

Yet, whereas prayers of communion are typically directed to a God
conceptualized as a transcendent Supreme Being, the word meditation is most often used by persons envisioning God as an immanent
spiritual presence. This may or may not amount to any real difference. For example, the Christian doctrine of the Trinity makes it possible to recognize simultaneously both God's transcendent attributes (i.e., God as Father and resurrected Son) and God's immanent
presence and activity in the world (i.e., God as Holy Spirit and the
Christian mystical tradition's references to the spiritual presence of
Christ). Likewise, Hinduism distinguishes between Nirguna and
Saguna Brahman, while Buddhism differentiates among the cosmic,
heavenly, and earthly "bodies" of the Buddha. But whatever the theological subtleties with which meditational systems might reconcile
their practices with the mainstream of religious thought, most depict
God in ways that border on pantheism. That is, they tend to understand God not so much as a Supreme Being ruling reality from
above, as an impersonal energy or consciousness nourishing the development of reality from within. The practical significance is that
God is understood as a dimension of depth within all natural processes; God, then, is an ever-present potential of experience. In this
view, God is thought to be present at the depth of human experience
and thus available to those who are willing to cultivate the appropriate life style and mental habits that shift awareness inward to its ultimate depth. When systems of religious thought view God as
transcendent they tend to believe that we are separated or estranged
from God through sin and disobedience. In contrast, placing emphasis upon God's immanence implies that the only barrier between us
and God is a self-imposed, psychological one that can gradually be
removed through conscientious effort. The route to God, then, can
be understood in primarily psychological terms. It is said that by
learning to relax, let go of everyday concerns, and cultivate inner re-
ceptivity, we can promote inner harmony with the divine spirit manifesting itself in the creative processes through which the universe
develops or unfolds. In this way meditation sets up the conditions for

an inflow of divine spirit into our lives and stimulates both healing and growth in each of the three major dimensions of our existence— the physical, mental, and spiritual. Meditation might be considered as a kind of privatized religious ritual. The phase of separation begins as we commence practices aimed at physical relaxation. In yoga, for example, specific bodily postures known as asanas are used to produce a state of deep relaxation. By sitting in comfortable positions, the entire physical system is gradually freed from signs of physiological stress or tension and induced into a state of calm and tranquility. Even simple meditational practices can cause the body's overall metabolic rate to drop about 25 percent.[12] Physiological changes produced by meditation include a substantial reduction in blood pressure, decrease in cardiac output, a lowered breathing rate, and an increase in the amount of alpha waves produced by the brain (a measure of rest and relaxation). In short, meditation restores the physical system to a state of calm equilibrium and thereby facilitates a rejuvenation of the body's resources for warding off fatigue and tension.

The induction of a state of physical relaxation signals the beginning of the marginal phase of the meditational process. The individual has quite literally removed him or herself from the concerns of everyday waking life. Sitting in quiet and relaxation she or he can let down normal defenses and temporarily let go of fears, worries, and problems. The meditational setting promotes a sense of safety, comfort, and well-being. The meditator enters this state of peacefulness in the expectation of harmonizing with the spiritual source of life's creativity, meaning, and purpose. For this reason meditation, as with prayers of communion, fosters mental and psychological growth. It enables us to replace gradually a limited self-image with a new identity forged from the experience of inner connection with a wider spiritual universe. The feeling of inward connection with a "higher" spiritual agency promotes the belief that one is less at the mercy of outer circumstances and more capable of being the creative center of one's life. All told, the quiet of meditation gives rise to a personal experience of what anthropologist Victor Turner calls "communitas"—a sense of sacred power somehow healing the strains of our secular life and reinvigorating us for responding to life with poise, love, and moral concern.

In addition to its physical and mental benefits, it should be obvious that meditation is also very much a spiritual experience. The act of temporarily setting aside our active will and habitual ways of thinking helps attune us to a range of feelings and sensations excluded from the normal waking state of consciousness. Those who are experienced at entering states of deep meditational relaxation report that less dominant aspects of consciousness become more pronounced. Aesthetic sensitivity, inspiration, intuition, and feelings of unity with other living beings all develop with repeated meditational experiences. Many meditators also speak of the opening of a "third eye," "sixth sense," or "still small voice" ordinarily covered over by the waking mind. That is, at some point in the meditational process there is a transition from absolute silence to a new and different kind of awareness. The deeper levels of meditation are said to afford an awareness of a transcendent reality which we call God, a timelessness we call eternity, and a sense of pure life we call light.

Meditation, by establishing an inner harmony with a sacred presence, becomes a pathway for revelatory insights concerning our place in the spiritual scheme of things. Among other things, meditational experiences tend to give rise to the belief that at the depth of our own individual selves we are identical with, or at least connected to, the divine ground or spirit underlying the created universe. This perception permanently expands an individual's understanding of the "natural laws and forces" thought to be governing reality. Such experiences imply that humans are potentially able to avail themselves of a metaphysical energy capable of stimulating growth and creativity in every dimension of their lives. Hence, upon completing a period of meditation and returning to or "reaggregating" their normal social identities, individuals feel renewed and strengthened. No longer identifying themselves simply in terms of socioeconomic structures, they begin to see themselves as "channels" through which a higher spiritual power finds worldly expression.

MINISTERING TO THE LIFE CYCLE

Religious communities come together not only to worship with one another but also to form a fellowship based upon shared values

and a common interpretation of life. Thus, the leadership or ministry of a religious congregation is entrusted with two somewhat separate tasks. The first has to do with officiating formal worship
services. The second has to do with incorporating persons into the
life of faith. Not only does the second of these entail the proclama-
tion of belief or doctrine, but it also includes activities of guidance
and counseling that comprise what is usually referred to as the "cure
of souls." The cure of souls has to do with assisting persons in handling the crises and conflicts that arise over the course of human life
in ways consonant with a distinctively religious perspective upon the
nature and meaning of human existence. In other words, it involves
bringing the resources and wisdom of religion to bear upon the developmental problems, emotional strains, and crises of will or meaning
that emerge throughout the life cycle.

The cure of souls is in many respects the religious counterpart to
modern systems of counseling and psychotherapy. The distinguishing characteristic of the cure of souls, however, is that the individual
understands his or her troubles as in some way disclosing the limit dimension of human existence. The cure of souls begins when an individual recognizes that his or her difficulties are insolvable in the
context of a purely rational conception of existence and thus turns to
the resources, wisdom, and authority of religion.[13] The cure of souls
has taken many forms throughout the history of world civilization.[14]
In ancient Israel, the Jewish community looked to wise men, scribes,
and rabbis for advice concerning how best to accord their lives with
God's will for humanity. In ancient Greece, philosophers were "physicians of the soul" and wove theology, philosophy, and psychology
into a comprehensive guide to the reasons for human suffering and
the secret to a balanced life. Hinduism and Buddhism have long relied on "holy men" of various kinds to serve as teachers or gurus for
those seeking assistance along the path to enlightenment. Modern
Westerners turn to ministers, priests, and rabbis for spiritual assistance in the form of pastoral guidance and counseling.

Historians William Clebsch and Charles Jaekle have identified
four separate functions that together represent the range of activities
associated with the cure of souls tradition. They write that the ministry of the cure of souls consists of helping acts, done by representative spiritual authorities, "directed toward the healing, sustaining,

guiding, and reconciling of troubled persons whose troubles arise in the context of ultimate meanings and concerns."[15] These four ministerial functions—healing, sustaining, guiding, and reconciling—all pertain directly to the patterning of individual lives according to the distinctively religious premise that our highest happiness and well-being are derived from a "higher," unseen order of things.

Healing, in the context of the religious cure of souls, involves restoring a person to wholeness in such a manner that this restoration achieves also a new level of spiritual insight and welfare. As opposed to secular healing activities, spiritual healings seek to help an individual gain insights and power over and beyond his or her condition prior to illness. Serious illness may, in this sense, prove to be a limit experience in that it prompts individuals to look beyond worldly resources and in some manner adapt themselves to a higher spiritual reality from which wholeness can be received. The means of spiritual healing vary between cultures and historical epochs. Exorcism, anointing with oil, pilgrimage to religious shrines, contact with relics, incantations performed by "medicine men" or shamans, and the laying on of hands by charismatic individuals have all served to effect physical cures while simultaneously expanding the patient's understanding of the "higher powers" of the universe. In our own day, there has been somewhat of a resurgence of interest in spiritual healing. Faith healing is popular not only in Protestant revival services but also in the Charismatic Movement among Roman Catholics. And, too, the so-called holistic health movement has introduced decidedly religious concepts concerning the healing process among medical professionals and the general public.[16] Holistic healing systems are predicated on the assumption that health is dependent on the balance and interplay among the physical, mental, and spiritual dimensions of our being. Advocates of holistic health embrace a variety of practices aimed at releasing the body's hidden healing powers, including exercise, meditation, and even techniques said to activate nonphysical or "spiritual" energies.

Sustaining consists of efforts to help a hurting person endure and transcend a circumstance in which restoration to his or her former condition is highly improbable. Following an amputation, severe economic reversal, or the death of a loved one, an individual must be helped to view his or her circumstances as still fraught with opportunities for spiritual growth. They must first be consoled and helped to gain sufficient hold of their lives as to protect themselves against further loss. They can then begin to find a new interpretation of their impoverished circumstances based upon a spiritual vision of their ultimate identity and purpose for living. A redemption of sorts is possible when they finally recover a positive outlook on life and identify possibilities for continued personal growth and achievement.

The function of guiding entails assisting perplexed persons to make confident choices between alternative courses of thought and action where these choices can be seen to affect both the present and future status of the soul. Scripture, sermons, and other means of religious instruction all offer individuals wisdom with which to pattern their lives according to the principles of spiritual development. Pastoral counseling and church discussion groups likewise help relate the world of human becoming to the ultimate meanings and purposes of life as discerned in revelatory experience. Religious guidance differs in an important way from secular forms of guidance and counseling in that it is based on the premise that the final sphere of human adaptation is the More or Beyond of physical existence. And thus although the cure of souls tradition may have nothing that is truly unique to bring to developmental issues such as autonomy, initiative, or industry, it is especially adept at guiding individuals to a successful resolution of crises that entail dimensions of trust, identity, meaning, or the acquisition of wisdom.

We might note in passing that moral guidance, as with effective ritualization, is intimately linked with developmental stages and virtues. Each of Erikson's eight adaptive strengths or virtues is developed in tension with alternative resolutions of the tasks that confront us in life. Thus, for example, the virtue of hope or faith is a personality strength meted out amidst experiences that might equally as well prompt a basic mistrust and such corollary "vices" as manipulativeness and gluttony. Similarly, it would be possible for lust to triumph over fidelity, indifference over care, or melancholy over wisdom. With this in mind, Capps has suggested that the rabbi, priest, or pastor is called upon to serve as "the moral counselor" even as he or she is called upon to act as a ritual coordinator.[17] Capps has proposed a convincing argument that what have traditionally been called "the seven deadly sins" represent impediments to character development and correspond to the eight stages of Erikson's model of the life cycle (Capps separates the traditional vice of sloth into its two components of indifference and melancholy, thereby arriving at eight "developmental vices"). Virtues and vices, of course, are not limited to chronological stages in that they continue to influence our capacity for mature interaction with others throughout the course of life. But they do have particular stages in which they have the best chance to develop. And they do build upon one another in a cumulative fashion and either limit or enhance the likelihood of the continued development of moral character. Capps argues that beginning in the first stage of life, the traditional sin of gluttony, or the tendency toward uncontrolled engorgement, is related to a fear or basic mistrust of the future and can thus be seen to be a principal impediment to the acquisition of hope. Likewise, anger (as an impediment to will), greed (purpose), envy (competence), pride (realistic identity and fidelity), lust (love), indifference (care), and melancholy (wisdom) all reveal the close connection between religion's historical concern for character formation and the requirements of successful human functioning across the life cycle. Moral counseling, it would appear, is not simply the stifling or crippling "moralizing" which many modern individuals have come to abhor about religion. Quite the contrary—responsible human becoming would appear to be intimately connected with the incorporation of individuals into a moral universe. Moral guidance serves the important cultural function of helping individuals pattern their commitments in ways most capable of building ongoing adaptive strengths for both themselves and the larger community.[18]

The final component of pastoral care, reconciliation, involves reestablishing broken relationships between individuals and their fellow human beings and between individuals and God. Following a prolonged personal crisis such as alcoholism, a criminal conviction, or traumatic argument, persons need to be helped to restore broken relationships with family members and with the wider community. And, too, persons need to feel that they have once again established a productive relationship with life's higher powers or God. One method of promoting reconciliation is offering forgiveness. Forgiveness overcomes walls of pride and hurt and lays the foundations for a new beginning freed from the barriers formerly separating us from one another or from God. Doctrines of grace, rituals of communion, and reminders to "forgive our trespasses" all communicate the forgiveness with which we are set free to begin anew. A second method through which religious ministry fosters reconciliation is the provision of spiritual discipline. The word discipline is often thought of as indicating punishment such as in the command to penance following confession of sins. But the larger sense of spiritual discipline refers to regulating life in ways that help prevent us from losing our intended path. Regular church attendance, the systematic study of scripture, and daily periods of prayer or meditation are all spiritual disciplines designed to help establish a harmonious relationship with God. Discipline, insofar as it reflects the lawful patterns by which human relationships are strengthened or by which we can achieve harmony with the More of ordinary conscious experience, is a necessary and beneficial element of productive human life.

Ministry, then, is an important cultural source of counseling and guidance. Owing to the fact that the religious cure of souls has as its fundamental premise the belief that the nature and meaning of human existence are disclosed as we approach the limit dimension of experience, it is well adapted to ministering to a good many human difficulties for which our modern secular therapies are of little or no help. And, for this reason, the various forms of ministry that comprise the world's living religious traditions have by no means become culturally outdated for modern individuals seeking helpful hints concerning the art of life cycle maintenance.

EPILOGUE

The purpose of this book has been to show the various ways in which human fulfillment depends upon values and experiences that have a broadly religious character. This view is, as we noted in the Introduction, somewhat at variance with the general drift of modern intellectual thought. The rapid advances made by the natural sciences around the turn of this century created a new intellectual environment dominated by the scientific method. A major consequence has been that the validity of an idea or belief has come to be judged almost solely upon the extent to which it is based upon empirical data. Religion, because it is usually associated with beliefs accepted on "faith" despite the lack of any empirical evidence, is usually viewed with great skepticism within the academic world. Nowhere is this more true than in the social sciences which established themselves in direct opposition to religious understandings of human nature. As epitomized in the writings of Marx and Freud, both sociology and psychology have inherent tendencies to view religion as a retrogressive force that stifles the full development of human potentials. For many modern intellectuals, then, religion is a subject matter to be shunned because it is thought both to be incapable of empirical proof and to represent an inferior way of approaching life's challenges.

By examining the life cycle in its totality, it becomes increasingly clear that any effort to study human nature empirically must acknowledge the fact that humans regularly, and even predictably, face developmental challenges that cannot be resolved through scientific methods of reasoning. Acquiring basic trust in life, questioning the meaning of one's life, deciding why one ought to be moral, sustaining self-worth in old age, and confronting one's own imminent death are all examples of commonly occurring human experiences that require the ability to take a religious or metaphysical perspective on life. This point was made eloquently by the noted sociologist Peter Berger when he began to realize in midcareer that the methods and antireligious biases of the social sciences had unfortunately caused them to exclude the most significant features of human existence. "The denial of metaphysics," he wrote, "may here be identified with the triumph of triviality."[1] For while social scientists have amassed voluminous amounts of quantitative information on a wide variety of subjects, they have categorically excluded the most profound questions and experiences that confront humanity both as individuals and as a species. Berger concluded that "a philosophical anthropology worthy of the name will have to regain a perception of these experiences and with this regain a metaphysical dimension."[2]

Berger has offered his own suggestions concerning how the social sciences might rediscover "ecstasy and metaphysics as crucial dimensions of human life." There are, he contends, any number of ordinary human events that occur in the "natural" world that appear to point beyond that reality. What he calls "signals of transcendence" fall within the empirically given human situation and thus demand to be included within the framework of modern intellectual thought. Yet, importantly, they show much of modern intellectual thought to be shortsighted in its premature attempt to exclude metaphysical considerations from empirical analyses of the nature and meaning of human life. Berger points specifically to the ways in which humanity's propensity for order, play, hope, condemnation, and humor reveals an implicit awareness of an ideal order of things that transcends the world of becoming.[3]

This book has developed the concept of the limit dimension of human experience in much the same spirit as Berger argued for the importance of "signals of transcendence." A fully empirical approach to understanding the nature of human fulfillment across the life cycle must take into account those experiences that induce us to adopt a distinctively religious orientation to life. Religion, far from being a solely retrogressive factor in human life, can function as a progressive force in guiding individuals toward growth and development. Chapter 1, while conceding that the type of religion that emerges in the process of primary socialization tends to be of the secondhand or immature variety, also noted the significant role religion potentially plays in helping young persons acquire personality strengths. Chapter 2 noted that belief or ideology is a necessary ingredient of identity formation and described the developmental processes whereby secondhand faith might give way to a type of religious orientation supportive of the fullest range of human potentials. The third and fourth chapters explored the many ways in which sustained growth and development in the second half of the life cycle depend upon our attainment of a spiritual perspective on issues of identity, meaning, death, and so forth. Chapter 5 examined the manner in which limit experiences of the positive or expansive type stimulate what Maslow calls "self-actualization" and disclose the further reaches of human nature. And, finally, chapter 6 maintained that by bringing the resources and vision born of encounters with the sacred to the task of ministry, organized religions embody a rich treasury of techniques for life cycle maintenance.

The general approach to the subject of religion sketched out in this book points the way to a style of religious thinking compatible with the empirical bent of modern thought. It is thus addressed especially to those readers who share many of the modern doubts about religion and find themselves questioning the importance or validity or religious beliefs. The "problem" of religious faith to an educated person living in the twentieth century is not the fact that there are other persons in the world who doubt the truth of his or her religious background. Rather, the problem of faith in the modern world is the persistence of certain doubts (e.g., about Bible miracles, whether there is one true religion, whether there is sufficient evidence to believe in a Supreme Being) even within those persons who have strong religious leanings. By defining religion in terms of the limit dimension of commonly recurring human experiences, religious thought gains an empirical foundation lacking in a faith based solely upon scripture. The subjective experience of encountering a More is, after all, as much a fact or datum as any other human experience. Religious thought can proceed from this fundamental datum of experience in an inductive fashion in much the same way as do the natural or social sciences. A major difference, of course, is that the More of religious experience is not an object or being in the physical universe. Hence religious thought is not properly concerned with issues of objective truth (that is, ascertaining the truth of a given proposition by experimental procedures utilizing the physical senses or technological extensions of these senses). What religious thought is interested in, then, is not the truth but rather the value of various beliefs. Religious beliefs are propositions about the nature and meaning of life as these are disclosed through experiences with the limit dimension of ordinary human awareness. It follows that the validity of religious beliefs is to be measured in terms of their ability to account for and guide individuals through the various limit experiences encountered throughout the life cycle.

The empirical or anthropological approach to religion takes life, not scripture or God, as its standard of value. That is, the only criteria that a humanistically oriented interpretation of religion has available to it are theoretical considerations of those forms of thought and behavior most likely to contribute to human well-being. William James, for example, suggested that immediate luminousness, philosophical reasonableness, and moral helpfulness are the only theoretical standards we have to measure religion against.[4] The criterion of immediate luminousness simply acknowledges the intrinsic value of religious experience and the positive quality it has in and of itself. We surely ought to value those experiences that carry with them an aura of happiness, exhilaration, or peace even if little else of measurable importance emanates from them. The second criterion, philosophical reasonableness, asks that religious beliefs never be irrational or run contrary to the sum total of things we know to be true about life. Even though religion proceeds from what may be called a nonrational or suprarational mode of consciousness, this does not warrant its interference with rationally and scientifically grounded knowledge of reality. An anthropological assessment of religion is surely justified in critiquing religion according to its capacity to be corational and coscientific.

The third and final criterion is that of moral helpfulness, by which

James meant the ability of a belief to lead us to productive relationships with the various spheres of life. This pertains most directly to the spirit of this book. As the famed Puritan preacher Jonathan Edwards acknowledged, "The degree in which our experience is productive of practice shows the degree in which our experience is spiritual and divine."[5] The final test of any belief is the way in which it leads us to a richer, more satisfying life. Religious beliefs are no exception to that rule. For this reason the notion of the life cycle is so important to religious reflection. If religion is not to be thought of as a separate compartment of life isolated from day-to-day existence, then we must be prepared to conceptualize how it interacts with the whole human developmental process from birth through death. It was with this in mind that Erikson's model of the eight virtues necessary to the successful patterning of the life cycle was proposed early in this book. Erikson's developmental model (or, for that matter, any comprehensive theory of psychosocial development) supplies useful criteria with which to assess the impact, or value, of religion upon human life. Insofar as religion fosters the development of some of these virtues (i.e., trust, identity, care, love, and wisdom) in a uniquely felicitous way, its value to the life cycle would appear to be established upon a firm empirical basis.

I suppose that in the final analysis the major issue at stake in any discussion of the nature and meaning of human life boils down to the question, What is the highest or most important sphere to which humans should adapt themselves? It is hoped that this book has made a case that human fulfillment cannot be understood totally in terms of our ability to adapt successfully to the social and economic spheres of life. Insofar as there are various moral and metaphysical contexts within which the life cycle unfolds, it would seem that any comprehensive account of the human enterprise must ultimately take seriously the religious hypothesis that, in the final analysis, wholeness is dependent upon the degree to which we can locate our lives within a wider spiritual environment.

NOTES

Introduction

1. David Tracy, *Blessed Rage for Order* (New York: Seabury Press, 1975).
2. William James, *The Varieties of Religious Experience* (New York: Collier Books, 1961), 377.

1. Religion and Childhood Development

1. Erik Erikson, *Insight and Responsibility* (New York: W. W. Norton, 1964), 165.
2. See the essays included in Peter Homans, ed., *Childhood and Selfhood: Essays on Tradition, Religion and Modernity in the Psychology of Erik H. Erikson* (Lewisburg, Pa.: Bucknell University Press, 1978); Carol Gilligan, *In a Different Voice: Psychological Theories and Women's Development* (Cambridge: Harvard University Press, 1982).
3. Gilligan, *In a Different Voice,* 170.
4. See P. Wolff, "The Developmental Psychologies of Jean Piaget and Psychoanalysis," in *Psychological Issues,* Monograph 5 (New York: International University Press, 1961); James Loder, "Convictional Knowing in Human Development," in *The Transforming Moment* (San Francisco: Harper & Row, 1982).
5. See John McDargh, *Psychoanalytic Object Relations Theory and the Study of Religion* (Lanham, Md.: University Press of America, 1983); Ana-Maria Rizzuto, *The Birth of the Living God* (Chicago: University of Chicago Press, 1979).

6. D. W. Winnicott, *Playing and Reality* (London: Tavistock Publications, 1971), 14.

7. Rizzuto, *Birth of the Living God,* 193.

8. This review of psychoanalytic objects relations theory is indebted to an excellent article by Mary Lou Randour and Julie Bondanza entitled "The Concept of God in the Psychological Formation of Females," *Psychoanalytic Psychology* 4 (1987): 301–13.

9. Rizzuto, *Birth of the Living God,* 47.

10. Gordon Allport, *The Individual and His Religion* (New York: Macmillan Co., 1950), 32.

11. William James, *The Varieties of Religious Experience* (New York: Collier Books, 1961), 24.

12. Walter Houston Clark, *The Psychology of Religion* (New York: Macmillan Co., 1958), 96–106.

13. See David Heller, *The Children's God* (Chicago: University of Chicago Press, 1986); Dora P. Chaplin, *Children and Religion* (New York: Charles Scribner's Sons, 1961); Merton Strommen, *Research on Religious Development* (New York: Hawthorn Books, 1971); Antoine Vergote, "Concept of God and Parental Images," *Journal for the Scientific Study of Religion* 8 (1969): 78–87.

2. Belief and Identity Formation

1. See the statistical findings reported in *Religion in America 1979–1980,* published by Princeton Religion Research Center; or Robert Hites, "Changes in Religious Attitudes During Four Years of College," *Journal of Social Psychology* 66 (1965): 51–63.

2. Erik Erikson, *History and the Historical Moment* (New York: W. W. Norton, 1975), 258.

3. Erik Erikson, *Young Man Luther* (New York: W. W. Norton, 1962), 222.

4. Ibid., 21.

5. Gordon Allport, *The Individual and His Religion* (New York: Macmillan Co., 1950), 83.

6. John A. T. Robinson, *Honest To God* (Philadelphia: Westminster Press, 1963).

7. Alfred Lord Tennyson, "In Memoriam A. H. H.," in *Collected Writings of Tennyson* (New York: Macmillan Co., 1896), 3:281.

8. Robinson, *Honest to God,* 7–28.

9. Paul Tillich, *Dynamics of Faith* (New York: Harper & Row, 1957).

10. Allport, *Individual and His Religion, 59–84.*

11. James, *The Varieties of Religious Experience* (New York: Collier Books, 1961), 50.

12. Allport, *Individual and His Religion,* 75.

13. James Fowler, "Faith, Liberation and Human Development." Paper delivered to Gammon Theological Seminary, February 1974.

14. James Fowler, *Stages of Faith* (San Francisco: Harper & Row, 1981).

3. Values and Midlife Transitions

1. The interested reader can find helpful discussions of adult developmental stages in Bernice Neugarten's *Middle Age and Aging* (Chicago: University of Chicago Press, 1968); Erik Erikson, ed., *Adulthood* (New York: W. W. Norton, 1978).

2. Daniel Levinson, *Seasons of a Man's Life* (New York: Alfred A. Knopf, 1978).

3. See Carol Gilligan, *In a Different Voice: Psychological Theory and Women's Development* (Cambridge: Harvard University Press, 1982).

4. See Gail Sheehy, *Passages* (New York: E. P. Dutton, 1976); George Valliant, *Adaptation to Life* (Boston: Little, Brown & Co., 1977); Maggie Scarf, "Husbands in Crisis," *McCalls,* June 1972.

5. Carl Jung, *Modern Man in Search of a Soul* (New York: Harcourt, Brace & World, 1933), 264.

6. Ibid., 106.

7. Many attempts have been made to conduct empirical research on religious dimensions of the developmental or aging process. Although the results of these studies vary somewhat according to the aspect of religion being measured, it nonetheless seems clear that the older we get, the more "religious" we become. Helpful reviews of the research on the religious aspects of the developmental psychology of aging can be found in David Moberg, "Religiosity and Old Age," *Gerontologist* 5 (1965): 78–87; E. Heenman, "Sociology of Religion and the Aged: the Empirical Lacunae," *Journal for the Scientific Study of Religion* 122 (1972): 171–76.

8. Erik Erikson, "Dr. Borg's Life Cycle," *Daedalus* 105 (1976): 11.

9. Ibid.

10. William James, "The Moral Philosopher and the Moral Life," in *The Will To Believe* (New York: Dover Publications, 1956), 211.

11. Ibid., 212.

12. Ibid., 213.

13. Alfred North Whitehead, quoted in Edward Brightman, *Philosophy of Religion* (New York: Prentice-Hall, 1940), 16.

14. Gordon Allport, *The Individual and His Religion* (New York: Macmillan Co., 1950), 75.

15. Lawrence Kohlberg, "Continuities in Childhood and Adult Moral Development Revisited," in P. Baltes and K. Schaie, eds., *Life-Span Development ~Psychology: Personality and Socialization* (New York: Academic Press, 1973), 202.

16. Ibid.

17. Ibid.

18. Viktor Frankl, *Man's Search For Meaning* (New York: Pocket Books, 1963), 164.

19. Ibid., 160.

20. Ibid., 166.

21. Ibid., 178.

22. Viktor Frankl, *The Unconscious God* (New York: Simon & Schuster, 1975), 61.

4. Aging, Dying, and Integrity

1. See Robert C. Peck, "Psychological Developments in the Second Half of Life," in Bernice Neugarten, ed., *Middle Age and Aging* (Chicago: University of Chicago Press, 1968).

2. See Robert N. Butler, "The Life Review: An Interpretation of Reminiscence in the Aged," in Lawrence R. Allman and Dennis T. Jaffe, eds., *Readings in Adult Psychology* (New York: Harper & Row, 1977), 329–39.

3. See Elliot Jacques, "Death and the Mid-Life Crisis," in Allman and Jaffe, eds., *Readings in Adult Psychology,* 315–26.

4. Sigmund Freud, "Thoughts for the Times on War and Death," cited in Jacques, "Death and the Mid-Life Crisis," 318.

5. Ibid.

6. Erik Erikson, *The Life Cycle Completed* (New York: W. W. Norton, 1982).

7. K. Brynolf Lyon, *Toward a Practical Theology of Aging* (Philadelphia: Fortress Press, 1985).

8. Erik Erikson, "Reflections on Dr. Borg's Life Cycle," *Daedalus* 105 (1976): 11.

9. Henri Nouwen and Walter Gaffney, *Aging: The Fulfillment of Life* (Garden City, N.Y.: Image Books, 1976), 36.

10. Ibid., 79

11. Han Fortmann, *Discovery of the East: Reflections on a New Culture,* quoted in Nouwen and Gaffney, *Aging,* 82–83.

12. Elisabeth Kubler-Ross, *On Death and Dying* (New York: Macmillan Co., 1969).

13. Ibid., 71.

14. Raymond A. Moody, *Life After Life* (New York: Bantam Books, 1976).

15. Ibid., 184.

16. Michael Sabom, *Recollections of Death: A Medical Investigation* (New York: Harper & Row, 1982).

17. Kenneth Ring, *Life at Death: A Scientific Investigation of the Near-Death Experience* (New York: Coward, McCann & Geoghegan, 1980).

18. Kenneth Ring, "Paranormal Aspects of Near-Death Experiences: Im-

plications for a New Paradigm." Paper delivered to the American Academy of Religion in Dallas, Texas, November 1980.

19. Elisabeth Kubler-Ross, interview in *People,* 24 Nov. 1975. See also James Crenshaw, "Interview with the Death and Dying Lady," *Fate* 30 (April 1977): 45–52.

20. Elisabeth Kubler-Ross, quoted in James Crenshaw, "Interview with the Death and Dying Lady," 45, 52.

5. Religion and Self-transcendence

1. See Abraham Maslow, *Toward a Psychology of Being* (New York: D. Van Nostrand, 1968); idem, *The Farther Reaches of Human Nature* (New York: Viking Press, 1971).

2. Maslow, *Toward a Psychology of Being,* 85.

3. Abraham Maslow, *Religions, Values, and Peak Experiences* (New York: Viking Press, 1970).

4. Ibid., x.

5. Ibid., 79, 66.

6. Ibid., 55, 56.

7. Maslow, *Toward a Psychology of Being,* 114.

8. Ibid., 154.

9. "Born Again," *Newsweek,* 25 Oct. 1976, 68–78.

10. The reader interested in psychological interpretations of conversion might wish to consult Edwin Starbuck, *The Psychology of Religion* (New York: Charles Scribner's Sons, 1903); Walter H. Clark, *The Psychology of Religion* (New York: Macmillan Co., 1958); Mary Jo Meadow and Richard Kahoe, *Psychology of Religion* (New York: Harper & Row, 1984).

11. William James, *The Varieties of Religious Experience* (New York: Collier Books, 1961), 160.

12. Charles Colson, cited in "Born Again," 75.

13. Jimmy Carter, quoted in H. Norton and B. Slosser, *The Miracle of Jimmy Carter* (Plainfield, N.J.: Logos International, 1976), 32.

14. Ibid., 36.

15. James, *Varieties of Religious Experience,* 198.

16. See Arthur J. Deikman, "Deautomization and the Mystic Experience," in Charles Tart, ed., *Altered States of Consciousness* (Garden City, N.Y.: Anchor Books, 1969), 25–46; Ernest Schactel's discussion of "secondary autocentricity" in his *Metamorphosis* (New York: Basic Books, 1959).

17. Richard M. Bucke, *Cosmic Consciousness* (New York: E. P. Dutton, 1969), 3.

18. Ibid., 10.

19. James, *Varieties of Religious Experience,* 220, 221.

20. Ibid., 211.

21. See ibid., 331–36.

22. Ibid., 335.

23. See Charles Tart, "Some Assumptions of Orthodox, Western Psychology," in his edited volume *Transpersonal Psychologies* (London: Routledge & Kegan Paul, 1975), 59–112.

24. See H. Guntrip, "Religion in relation to personal integration," *The British Journal of Medical Psychology* 42 (1969): 323–33.

25. William James, "Reflex Action and Theism," in *The Will To Believe* (New York: Dover Publications, 1956), 127.

26. Ibid.

27. A helpful discussion of this issue can be found in James Loder, "Convictional Knowing in Human Development," in his *The Transforming Moment* (San Francisco: Harper & Row, 1981).

6. Religion and the Art of Life Cycle Maintenance

1. Rufus Jones, *The World Within,* quoted in Richard Streng's excellent text *Understanding Religious Life* (Encino, Cal.: Dickenson Publishing Co.), 78.

2. Victor Turner, *The Ritual Process* (Ithaca, N.Y.: Cornell University Press, 1977).

3. A helpful illustration of how rites of passage help structure the life cycle in accordance with religious patterns and meanings is the ceremony of marriage or holy matrimony. The moment of engagement or betrothal marks the individual's separation from his or her former status as a single person. The couple is no longer part of the pool of "available" young men and women free to pursue new romantic relationships. The marginal phase begins with religious instruction from a minister, priest, or rabbi. Advice is given about resolving marriage difficulties in a way consistent with the congregation's religious and moral beliefs. The marginal phase culminates in a religious ceremony fraught with symbols of communitas. Entering into a holy sanctuary dressed in ritual clothing, the couple approach an altar bedecked with religious symbols. An ordained clergy stands before them representing the spiritual presence of God. They expectantly gaze upon one another as they are told that they are forming "a union" in which "two become one." The implicit symbolism of the ceremony fosters the sense that their two personalities have somehow been forged together into a new and higher synthesis. In a Christian church, for example, there are any number of symbolic representations of the possibility of a higher union of persons: the notion of the Trinity suggests that three persons can have one identity; the church is itself a "body" composed not only of Christ but of all the church members; and the entire message of Christ's life is the higher good to be achieved by putting others before yourself through sacrificial love. The religious ceremony signifies that the two individuals are not simply entering

into a legal contract but rather into a holy covenant to which God is witness. Because the two are covenanting not only with one another but also with God, their union has a spiritual dimension that transcends the ups and downs of human life (i.e., in sickness and in health, for better or for worse). The rings exchanged symbolize unbroken connection, wholeness, and fidelity. Their vows note that marriage is not to be viewed in terms of material costs and benefits but as part of a human's responsibility for adhering to divine will and purpose. Prayer, scripture reading, and a final blessing by the officiating minister of God all invoke the sense of a higher spiritual power entering into the lives of the marriage couple and ennobling them for the tasks ahead. As they turn to head back down the aisle and assume their new roles and status in the structures of society, they do so having been fortified and invigorated by the living spirit of communitas.

4. Sigmund Freud, "Obsessive Acts and Religious Practices," in *The Standard Edition of the Complete Works of Sigmund Freud,* ed. James Strachey (London: Hogarth Press, 1959), 9:115–27.

5. See Erik Erikson, *Toys and Reasons: Stages in the Ritualization of Experience* (New York: W. W. Norton, 1977); idem, *The Life Cycle Completed* (New York: W. W. Norton, 1982).

6. Erikson, *Toys and Reasons, 91.*

7. Donald Capps, *Life Cycle Theory and Pastoral Care* (Philadelphia: Fortress Press, 1982), 60. A good deal of this section is dependent upon Capps's insightful book and readers are encouraged to study his discussion of Erikson's work on rituals as a resource for pastoral care.

8. M. G. Ross, *Religious Beliefs of Youth,* cited in Walter Houston Clark, *The Psychology of Religion* (New York: Macmillan Co., 1958), 307–27.

9. Ibid.

10. Ibid.

11. Nels Ferre, quoted in Streng, *Understanding Religious Life,* 78.

12. See "Transcendental Meditation," in John White, ed., *The Highest State of Consciousness* (Garden City, N.Y.: Anchor Press, 1972).

13. This entire section is heavily indebted to the superb study by William Clebsch and Charles Jaekle entitled *Pastoral Care in Historical Perspective* (New York: Jason Aronson, 1964).

14. See John T. McNeill, *A History of the Cure of Souls* (New York: Harper & Row, 1951).

15. Clebsch and Jaekle, *Pastoral Care,* 4.

16. See Robert C. Fuller, "Unorthodox Medicine and American Religious Life," *Journal of Religion* 67 (January 1987): 50–65.

17. See Capps, "The Moral Counselor," in *Life Cycle Theory and Pastoral Care.*

18. An excellent discussion of the ethical dimensions of guidance and counseling can be found in Don Browning, *The Moral Context of Pastoral Care* (Philadelphia: Westminster Press, 1976).

Epilogue

1. Peter Berger, *A Rumor of Angels* (Garden City, N.Y.: Anchor Books), 75. See also his *The Heretical Imperative: Contemporary Possibilities of Religious Affirmation* (Garden City, N.Y.: Anchor Press, 1979). I have reviewed and offered critical commentary on Berger's "empirical" approach to religion in an article entitled "Religion and Empiricism in the Works of Peter Berger" in *Zygon* 22 (December 1987): 497–510.

2. Ibid.

3. Ibid.

4. William James, *The Varieties of Religious Experience* (New York: Collier Books, 1961), 33.

5. Jonathan Edwards, quoted in ibid., 35.

SUGGESTED READING

Introduction

A helpful sourcebook of Marx's views on religion is *Karl Marx and Friedrich Engels: On Religion* (New York: Schocken Books, 1964). The views of Freud presented in this chapter barely scratch the surface of his complex and nuanced interpretations of religion. The best place to begin a study of Freud's views on religion is with his *The Future of an Illusion* (New York: Anchor Books, 1961) and his article entitled "Obsessive Acts and Religious Practices," which can be found in *The Standard Edition of the Complete Works of Sigmund Freud,* ed. James Strachey (London: Hogarth Press, 1959), 9:115–27. Further studies should include Freud's books entitled *Totem and Taboo* (New York: W. W. Norton, 1961); and *Moses and Monotheism* (New York: Vintage Books, 1967). Excellent works interpreting Freud's legacy for the study of religion include Peter Homans, *Theology After Freud* (Indianapolis: Bobbs-Merrill, 1970) and Philip Rieff, *The Triumph of the Therapeutic* (New York: Harper & Row, 1966).

A good introductory text which examines problems in the definition and study of religion is Frederick Streng, *Understanding Religious Life* (Encino, Ca.: Dickenson Publishing Co., 1976). There are, of course, any number of excellent works that offer a more sophisticated analysis of religion from what might be called a postmodern point of view. Highly recommended is David Tracy, *Blessed Rage for Order* (New York: Seabury Press, 1975). Ian Barbour, *Myths, Models, and Paradigms: A Comparative Study in Science and Religion* (San Francisco: Harper & Row, 1974) provides a thoughtful study of the relationship between religion and science. Don Browning, *Religious Thought and the Modern Psychologies* (Philadelphia: Fortress Press,

1987) is an authoritative exposition of the religious and moral dimensions of social scientific thinking.

1. Religion and Childhood Development

Readers looking for introductory texts in the area of childhood development might wish to consult Robert Kegan, *The Evolving Self: Problem and Process in Human Development* (Cambridge: Harvard University Press, 1982) or Henry Maier, *Three Theories of Child Development* (New York: Harper & Row, 1969).

The brief comments concerning gender differences in psychological development might be pursued by reading Carol Gilligan, *In a Different Voice: Psychological Theory and Women's Development* (Cambridge: Harvard University Press, 1982); Mary Belenky et al., *Women's Ways of Knowing: The Development of Mind, Voice, and Self* (New York: Basic Books, 1986); Mary Lou Randour and Julie Bondanza, "The Concept of God in the Psychological Formation of Females," *Psychoanalytic Psychology* 4 (1987): 301–13.

The best places to begin a careful reading of Erik Erikson's works are his *Insight and Responsibility* (New York: W. W. Norton, 1964); *Identity: Youth and Crisis* (New York: W. W. Norton, 1968); *Childhood and Society* (New York: W. W. Norton, 1963). The best secondary works on Erikson's theories of religion are Don Browning, *Generative Man* (New York: Delta Books, 1975); and J. Eugene Wright, *Erikson: Identity and Religion* (New York: Seabury Press, 1982).

Informative studies of childhood religion include Ana-Maria Rizzuto, *The Birth of the Living God* (Chicago: University of Chicago Press, 1979); David Heller, *The Children's God* (Chicago: University of Chicago Press, 1986); Gordon Allport, *The Individual and His Religion* (New York: Macmillan Co., 1950).

2. Belief and Identity Formation

Sharon Parks, *The Critical Years: The Young Adult Search for a Faith to Live By* (San Francisco: Harper & Row, 1986) is a reliable overview of themes in adolescent faith development. Erik Erikson's study of the ideological struggles related to identity formation in his *Young Man Luther* (New York: W. W. Norton, 1962) remains a classic in the psychological study of religion.

A provocative essay concerning the role of doubt in faith development is Paul Tillich, *The Dynamics of Faith* (New York: Harper & Row, 1957). Two works that help portray the close relationship of religious turbulence to the development of a mature faith are Augustine's *Confessions* (New York: E. P. Dutton, 1932); and Malcolm X, *The Autobiography of Malcolm X* (New York: Grove Press, 1964).

Without question the most noted academic treatments of the pragmatic validation of faith are William James's essays "The Will to Believe," "Reflex Action and Theism," and "The Moral Philosopher and the Moral Life," in his *The Will to Believe* (New York: Dover Publications, 1956). His essay "Pragmatism and Religion," in *Pragmatism* (New York: Meridian Books, 1974) gives additional perspective as to how one might assess the pragmatic foundations and meaning of religious faith. James has, moreover, given one of the most eloquent expositions of the mystical validation of faith in the concluding section of his famous *The Varieties of Religious Experience* (Cambridge: Harvard University Press, 1985); and in his *A Pluralistic Universe* (New York: E. P. Dutton, 1971).

The best sources for James Fowler's studies of faith development are his *Stages of Faith: The Psychology of Human Development and the Quest for Meaning* (San Francisco: Harper & Row, 1981); James Fowler and Sam Keen, *Life Maps: Conversations on the Journey of Faith* (Waco, Tex.: Word, 1978).

3. Values and Midlife Transitions

A good many studies of adult development have appeared in recent years. Among the most noted are Bernice Neugarten, *Middle Age and Aging* (Chicago: University of Chicago Press, 1968); Erik Erikson, *Adulthood* (New York: W. W. Norton, 1978); Daniel Levinson, *Seasons of a Man's Life* (New York: Alfred A. Knopf, 1978); George Valliant, *Adaptation to Life* (Boston: Little, Brown & Co., 1977); Gail Sheehy, *Passages* (New York: E. P. Dutton, 1976).

Jung's writings have profoundly influenced the literature on adult developmental processes. Readers interested in Jung's work might wish to begin with his autobiography, *Memories, Dreams, Reflections* (New York: Vintage Books, 1965), in which he reveals the religious aspects of his own life, and then proceed to such works as *Two Essays on Analytical Psychology* (Princeton: Princeton University Press, 1966); *Psychology and Religion* (New Haven: Yale University Press, 1974); *Modern Man in Search of a Soul* (New York: Harcourt, Brace & World, 1933). Applications of Jung's theories in the study of the religious dimensions of personality development include Ira Progoff, *The Symbolic and the Real* (New York: Julian Press, 1963); idem, *Depth Psychology and Modern Man* (New York: Julian Press, 1959); June Singer, *Boundaries of the Soul* (Garden City, N.Y.: Anchor Books, 1974); Joseph Campbell, *Hero with a Thousand Faces* (New York: Pantheon Books, 1949); Edward Whitmont, *The Symbolic Quest* (New York: G. P. Putnam's Sons, 1969).

4. Aging, Dying, and Integrity

Both Steven H. Zarit, ed., *Readings in Aging and Death* (New York: Harper & Row, 1982); and Lawrence Allman and Dennis Jaffe, eds., *Readings in Adult Psychology: Contemporary Perspectives* (New York: Harper & Row, 1977) provide helpful collections of essays on a variety of topics related to psychological development in old age. Erik Erikson's *The Life Cycle Completed* (New York: W. W. Norton, 1982) helps correct the overemphasis upon the early years of development found in most of his writings by concentrating on the latter years of the life cycle.

An excellent theological analysis of aging can be found in K. Brynolf Lyon, *Toward a Practical Theology of Aging* (Philadelphia: Fortress Press, 1985). Also highly recommended as a starting point for theological reflection on the aging process is Don Browning, "Preface to a Practical Theology of Aging," *Pastoral Psychology* 24 (1975): 151–67. Examples of broader treatments of the ways in which human development might be viewed in religious ways are James Lapsley's insightful *Salvation and Health: The Interlocking Processes of Life* (Philadelphia: Westminster Press, 1972); and Gregory Baum, *Man Becoming: God in Secular Experience* (New York: Seabury Press, 1979).

The possibility that dying individuals have experiences that might provide clues about the afterlife or metaphysical dimensions of reality has long intrigued the human race. *The Tibetan Book of the Dead,* actually a book recording the experiences of individuals adept at entering meditational trance states which were thought to be similar to the states entered at death, is a classic in this area of human thought and speculation. Recent books such as Raymond Moody, *Life After Life* (New York: Bantam Books, 1976); Michael Sabom, *Recollections of Death: A Medical Investigation* (New York: Harper & Row, 1982); Kenneth Ring, *Life at Death: A Scientific Investigation of the Near-Death Experience* (New York: Coward, McCann & Geoghegan, 1980); Stanislav Grof, *The Human Encounter with Death* (New York: E. P. Dutton, 1977); Elisabeth Kubler-Ross, *Death: The Final Stage of Growth* (Englewood Cliffs, N.J.: Prentice-Hall, 1975) have stimulated Americans' curiosity about the possible transcendental aspects of the dying process.

5. Religion and Self-transcendence

William James, *The Varieties of Religious Experience* (Cambridge: Harvard University Press, 1985) remains the single best discussion of religious experience to this day. James expanded upon these points in both the concluding section of his *A Pluralistic Universe* (New York: Dutton, 1971) and an essay entitled "A Suggestion about Mysticism," in *Collected Essays and Reviews,* ed. Ralph Barton Perry (New York: Longmans, Green & Co., 1911), 500–513.

James Loder, *The Transforming Moment: Understanding Convictional Experiences* (San Francisco: Harper & Row, 1981) is a lucid attempt to show

how religious experiences relate to other structures of human knowing and human development. Readers might also wish to consult significant texts in the "altered states of consciousness" field such as Robert Ornstein, *The Psychology of Consciousness* (San Francisco: W. H. Frieman & Co., 1972); Charles Tart, *States of Consciousness* (New York: E. P. Dutton, 1975), or almost any issue of *The Journal of Transpersonal Psychology.*

6. Religion and the Art of Life Cycle Maintenance

The most helpful assessment of the "cure of souls" or "pastoral counseling" dimension of religion in light of developmental psychology is Donald Capps, *Life Cycle Theory and Pastoral Care* (Philadelphia: Fortress Press, 1983). Jay Wilcoxen, "Some Anthropocentric Aspects of Israel's Sacred History," *Journal of Religion* 48 (October 1968): 333–50 offers a splendid interpretation of Western biblical materials as themselves rooted in the practical concerns of guiding human development. Other well-known assessments of the "cure of souls" trâdition include John T. McNeill, *A History of the Cure of Souls* (New York: Harper & Row, 1951); Charles Jaekle and William Clebsch, *Pastoral Care in Historical Perspective* (New York: Jason Aronson, 1975).

Individuals wishing to pursue the psychological study of religious practices such as prayer, worship, and so forth might begin by consulting the overviews and extensive bibliography in Mary Jo Meadow and Richard Kahoe, *Psychology of Religion* (New York: Harper & Row, 1984).

Epilogue

Peter Berger's efforts to elucidate the "signals of transcendence" in human experience are a significant expression of the kind of religious thought compatible with the point of view taken in this book. Berger's attempts to revive a style of Christian religious thought pioneered by Schleiermacher (and which has its parallels in many Hindu and Buddhist theological traditions) can be found in his *A Rumor of Angels* (Garden City, N.Y.: Anchor Books, 1969); and *The Heretical Imperative* (Garden City, N.Y.: Anchor Books, 1979). I have reviewed and offered critical commentary on Berger's work in an article entitled "Religion and Empiricism in the Works of Peter Berger," *Zygon* 22 (December 1987): 497–510.

Volume 3 of Paul Tillich, *Systematic Theology* (Chicago: University of Chicago Press, 1967) provides a very suggestive model for envisioning how the various orders of human existence participate in, and contribute to, the divine life. In his preface to the third volume, Tillich acknowledges his indebtedness to Teilhard de Chardin, *The Phenomenon of Man* (New York: Harper & Row, 1961). Although most of Teilhard's "science" is seriously out of date, his capacity to envision the whole of biological evolution in a spiritual vein remains one of this century's most important efforts to forge a coscientific system of religious thought. In addition to Gregory Baum, *Man Becoming: God in Secular Experience* (New York: Seabury Press, 1979), readers might wish to consult the writings of Karl Rahner, David Tracy, and Langdon Gilkey in that all three aim to elucidate a theological anthropology (i.e., a comprehensive model of human nature which builds upon the various sciences in such a way as to provide a nonreductionistic account of humanity's religious nature). This is, of course, also the aim of the many so-called process theologians such as Schubert Ogden, Charles Hartshorne, John Cobb, and Alfred North Whitehead.

INDEX

Allport, G., ix, 29, 39, 40, 67
  theory of mature religiosity,
    47–51

Belief
  emergence of religious, 27–28
  firsthand vs. secondhand, 31
Berger, P., 137
Bucke, R. M., 107

Capps, D., 123, 133–34, 147 n. 7
Childhood, immaturity of beliefs
  during, 32–33
Clark, W. H., 32–33, 124
Clebsch, W., 131
Conversion, 101–6
Creativity as stimulated by
  religion, 27–28, 100

Detachment, 81
Doubt
  as related to mature faith,
    40–43
  types of, 41–43

Edwards, J., 140

Erikson, E., 16–24, 65, 66, 75, 79,
  82, 114, 133, 140
  differences from Freud of, 16–17
  eight developmental virtues as
    tests of the value of religion,
    140
  eight stages of development,
    19–24, 36–38, 57–59, 77–78
  theory of ritualization, 122–23
Ethics and religious faith, 49–50,
  66–68

Fairbairn, W. R., 112
Faith
  Allport's theory of mature faith,
    47–51
  developed through doubt, 40–47
  firsthand vs. secondhand, 31–33,
    40, 48
  Fowler's theory of faith
    development, 51–55
  ideological functions of, 39–40,
    47
  need for experiential foundations
    in, 51
  as a verb, 44–45, 52

Feminist issues in developmental
theory, 19, 52, 150
Ferre, N., 126
Fortmann, H., 83
Fowler, J., 71
theory of faith development,
51–55
Frankl, V., 69–71
Freud, S., 3–4, 14–17, 26, 27,
75–76, 112, 136
on prayer, 124–25
on rituals, 122
Fulfillment, 27–28, 38–39, 56, 65,
66–68, 71–73, 81–82, 90–91,
106, 109, 111–12, 137

Gaffney, W., 80
Gilligan, C., 19, 60
God
as projection of psychological
needs, 4, 15–16
as component of psychological
development, 26–28
Guntrip, H., 113

Hindu model of the life cycle,
65–66
Hope, 21, 81

Identity issues and religious
commitment, 33–40, 99–100
Ideology and religious thought,
37–40, 47
Institutional religion
psychological criticisms of, 3–4,
14–16, 97–98
as socialization agent, 16,
117–21, 123–24, 130–35
as source of doubt, 42–43
as transformative agent, 28–31,
116
Intellectual validation of faith, 46

Jaekle, C., 131

James, W., 49, 51, 103, 113, 114
definition of religion, 11
on the distinction between
firsthand and secondhand
faith, 31
on the strenuous mood, 66–67
tests of the value of religious
experiences, 139–40
views of mysticism, 108–9

Jones, R., 118
Jung, C. G., 62, 63, 64–65, 115

Klein, M., 112
Kohlberg, L., 108
theory of relationship between
religion and moral
development, 67–68
Kubler-Ross, E., 86–90, 94–95

Levinson, D., 60, 62
Limit experience
as clue to the religious dimension
of human nature, 10, 111–15
defined, 10
disclosing life's "higher" reaches,
96, 98–101
in midlife, 62–66, 71–72
relevance of for philosophical
anthropology, 111–15, 137–38
role of in fostering firsthand
faith, 88–89, 111
significance of for adaptation,
11–12, 25, 106, 114–15
Lyon, K. B., 78

Marx, K., 3–4, 48, 136
Maslow, A., 97–101, 118
Meaning as grounded in religion,
69–71
Meditation, 127–30
Midlife crises as limit experiences,
62–66, 72–73
Moody, R., 90–93, 94

Mysticism, 106–9
  role of in moral development,
    68
  role of in validating faith, 46
  as source of faith, 51
  as source of wisdom, 82–83

Near-death experiences, 91–95
Nouwen, H., 80

Object relations theory, 25–26
  and the idea of God, 26–28
  on the integrating character of
    religion, 112–15
Otto, R., 8–9, 99

Piaget, J., 34, 51
Pragmatic validation of faith, 45,
    139–40
Prayer, 4, 88
  considered psychologically,
    124–27
  as imitated behavior, 28–29
Psychology, inherent difficulty of
    with religion, 3–4, 7, 16, 41,
    109–11

Religion. *See also* Institutional
    religion
  contrasted with secularism, 2–5,
    41–42, 110
  as a form of adaptation to life's
    developmental challenges,
    11–12, 66–68, 71–73, 81–83,
    90–91, 106, 109, 111–15
  formal definitions of, 8–9
  functional definitions of, 9, 117
  and moral commitment, 49–50,
    66–68
  and psychological
    transformation, 99–101,
    105–7, 111–15, 117
  as a retrogressive force in life,
    3–4, 15–17, 22

and transitions between
    developmental stages, 114–15
Ring, K., 93–94
Rites of passage, 121
Rizzuto, A., 27–28
Robinson, J., 42, 44

Sabom, M., 92–94
Scientific method
  as a challenge to religion, 3,
    41–42
  limits of in studying humanity's
    spiritual nature, 5–6, 97,
    110–11, 137
Secularism as a challenge to
    religion, 4–5, 110
Signals of transcendence, 137
Socialization processes and
    religion, 16, 28–31
Stage theory and ministry, 23, 24,
    30, 117, 122–24, 133–34
Strenuous mood as nourished by
    religion, 66

Tennyson, A., 44
Tillich, P., 44–45
Tracy, D., 10
Transpersonal aspects of human
    development, 65, 71, 79,
    99–101, 105, 112, 114–15
Turner, V., 118–19, 129

Unconscious
  as source of meaning, 71
  as source of religious experience,
    65, 71, 105

Value of religious beliefs, 139
Vision, 82–84, 90
Vocation and religious faith, 64

Winnicott, D. W., 26–27, 112
Wisdom, 78, 81, 90
Wisdom literature, 84, 153
Worship as a limit experience, 84